pretext

Chocolate Factory
Paris

Paul McCarthy

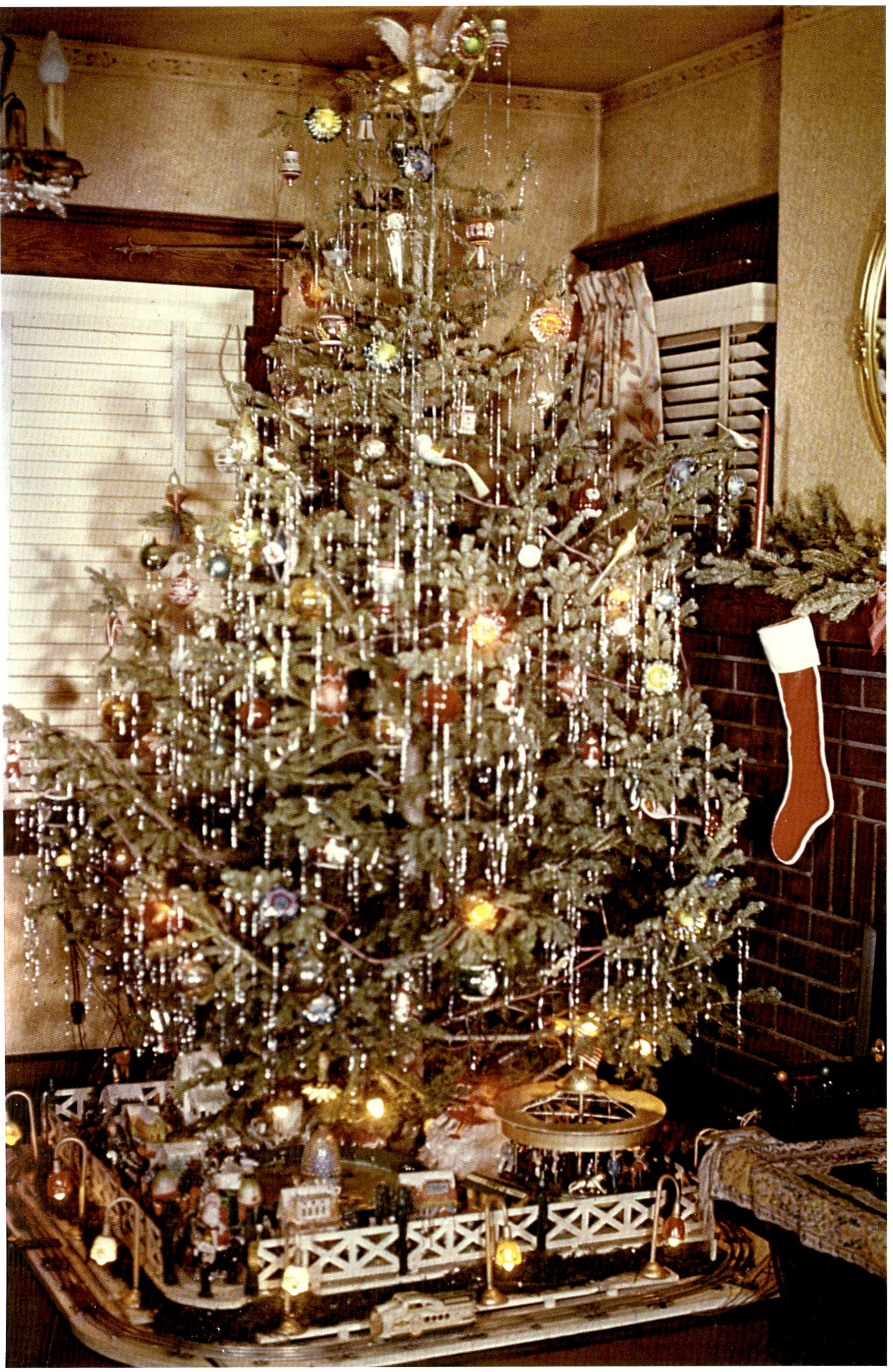

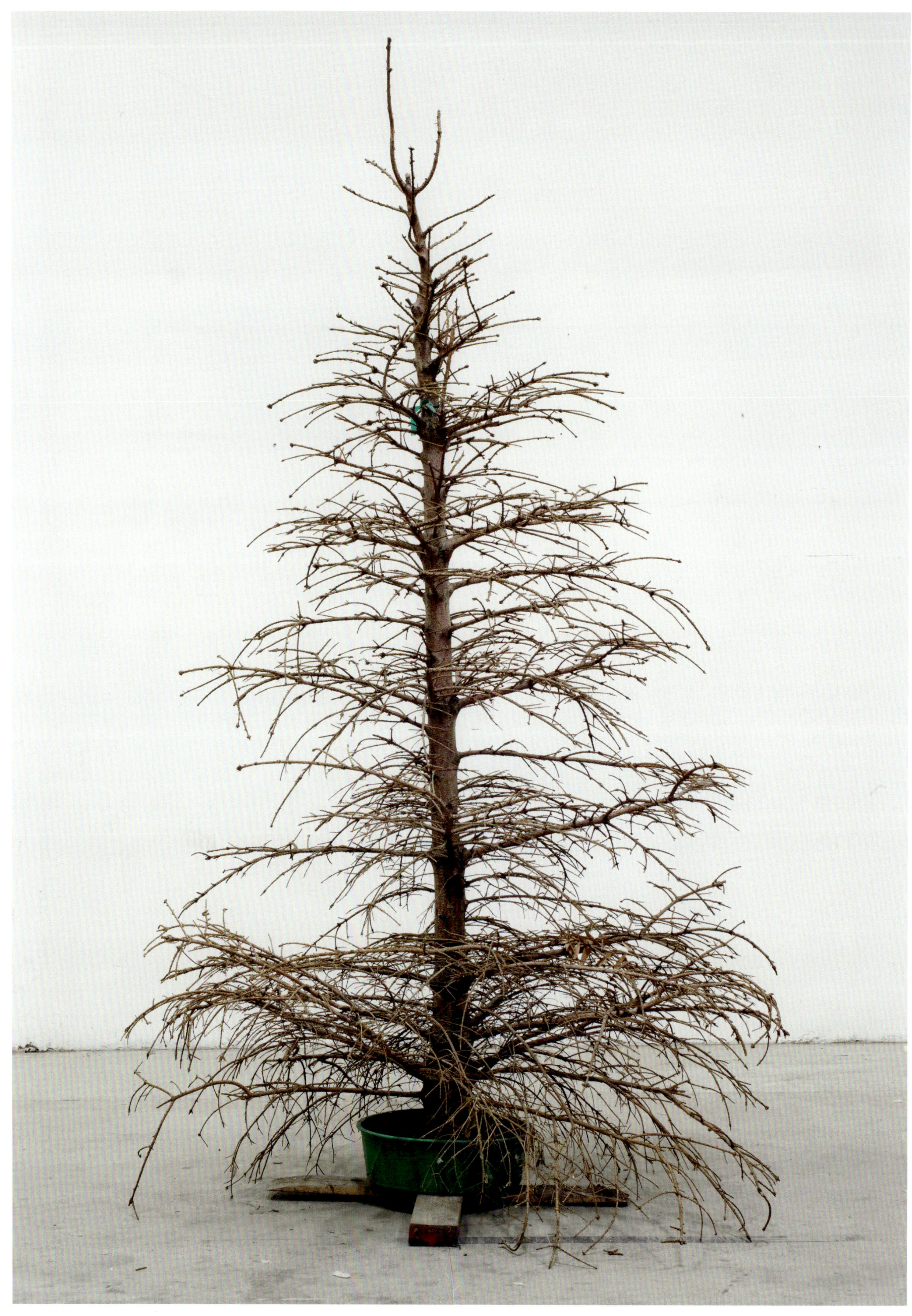

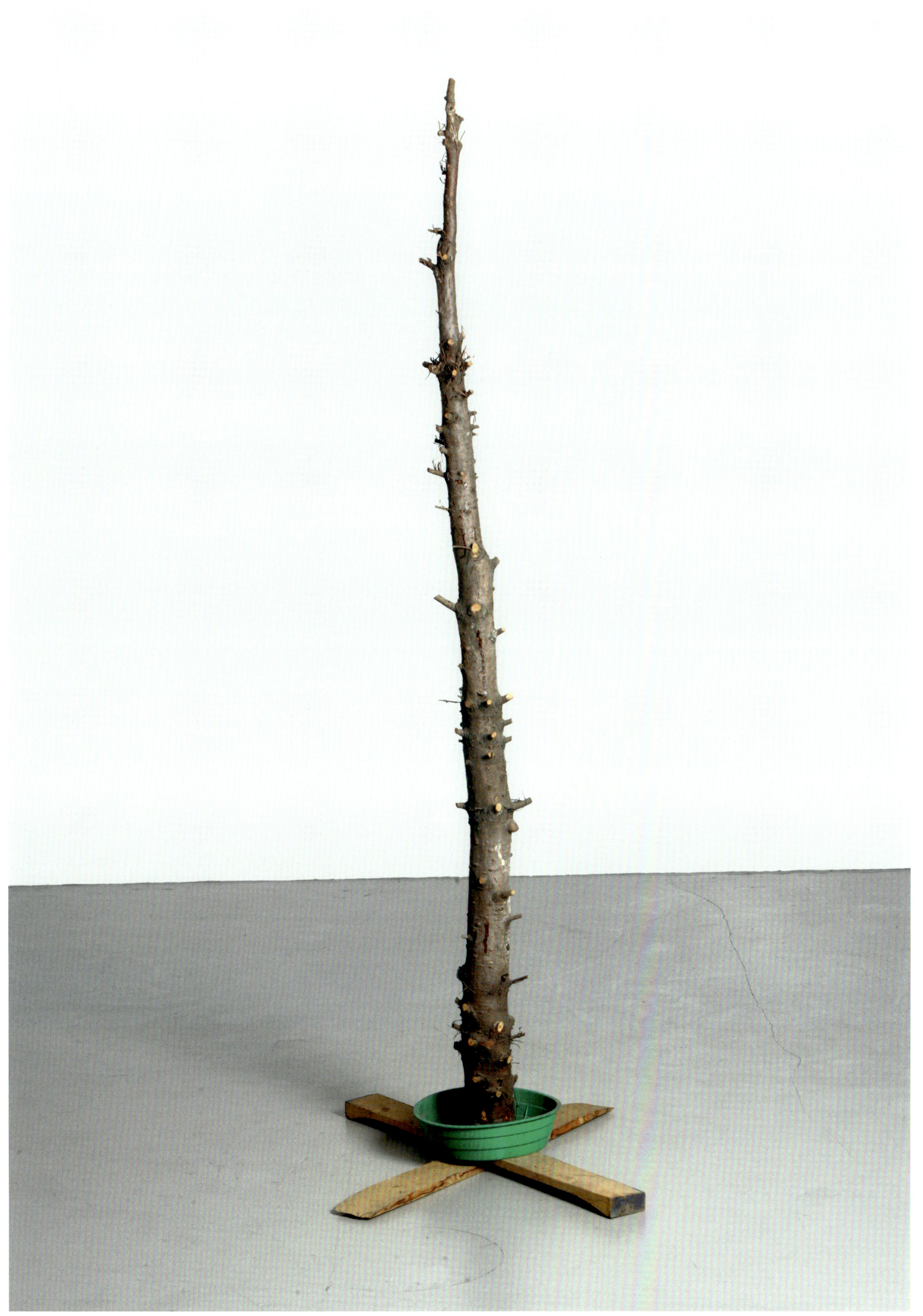

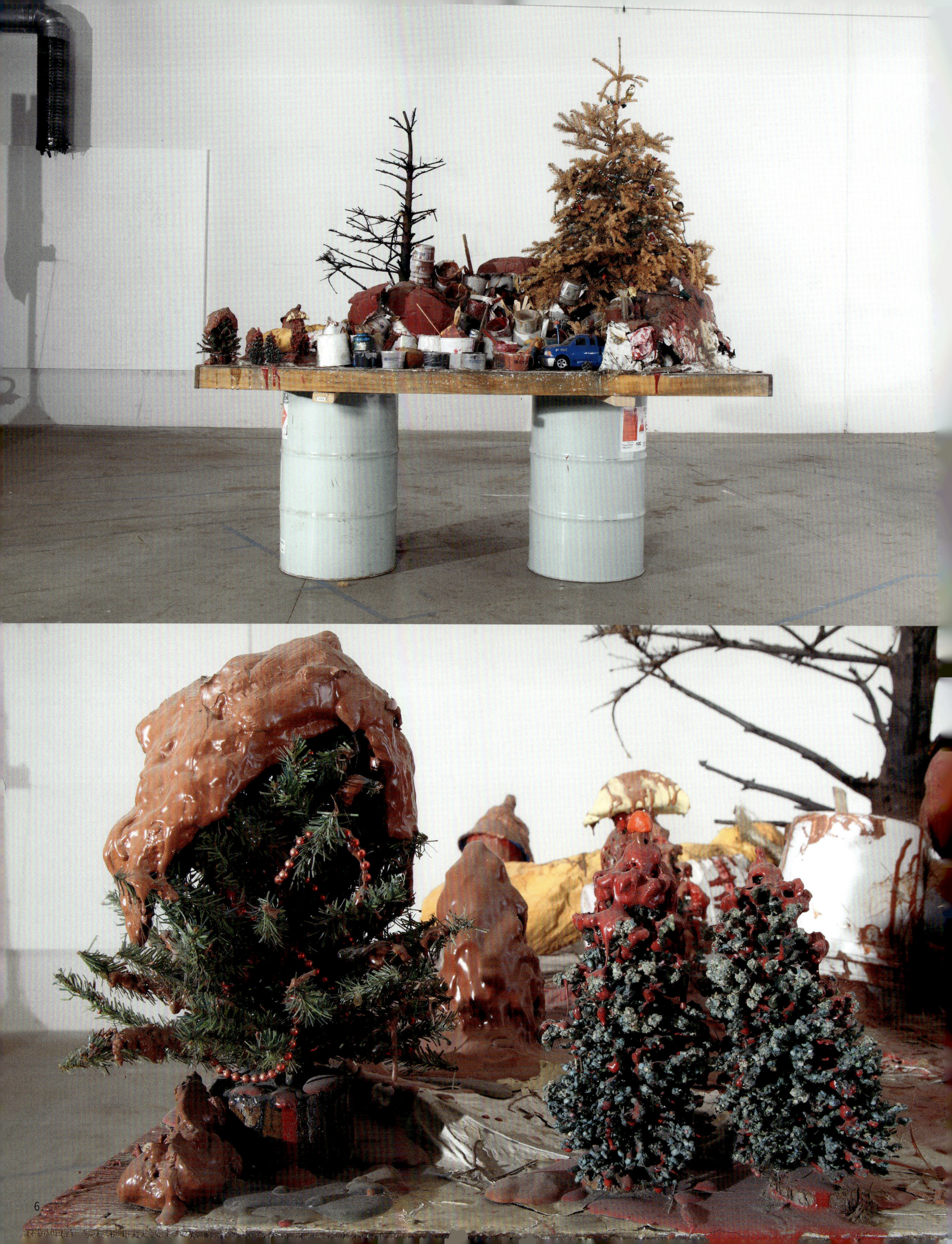

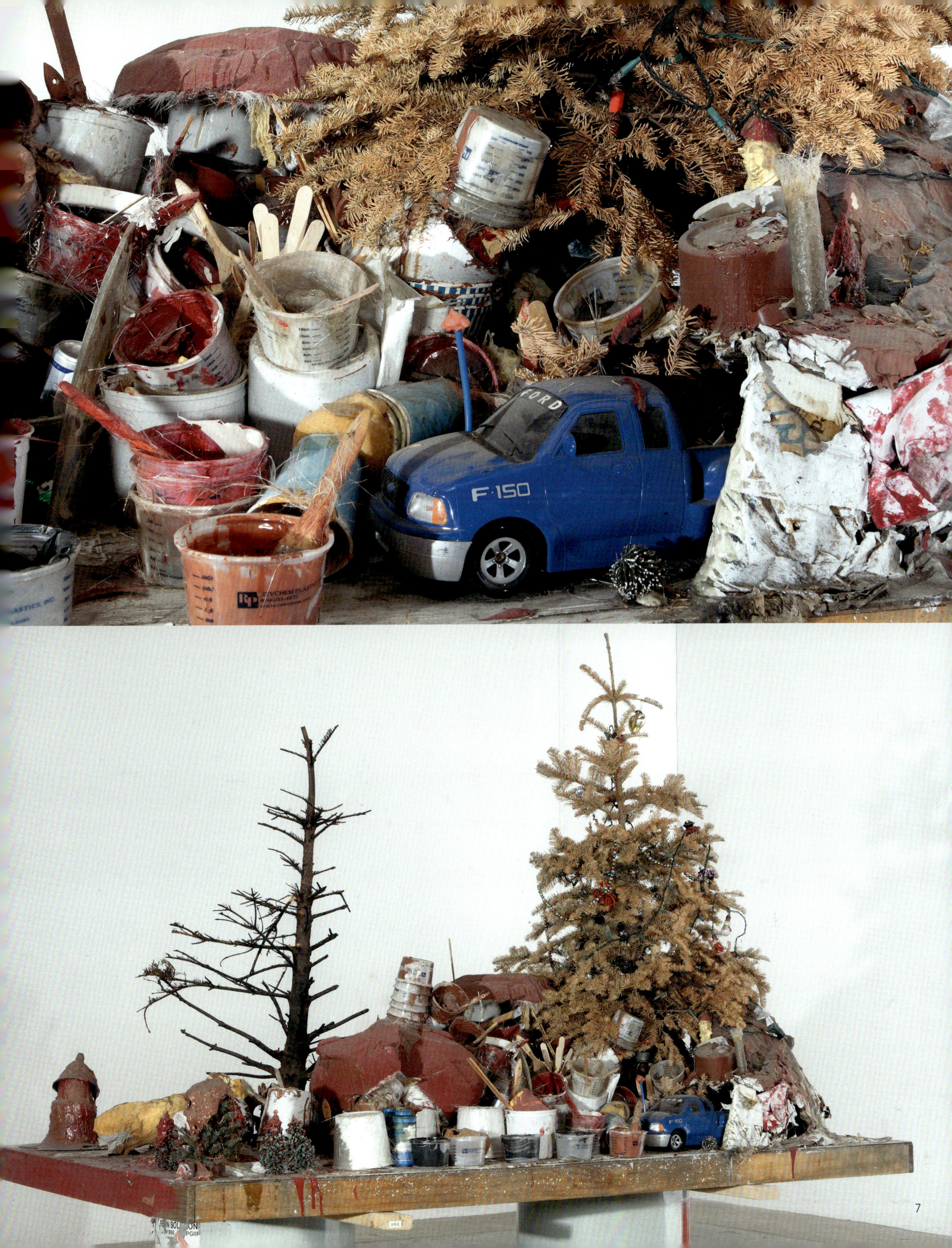
FORD
F·150

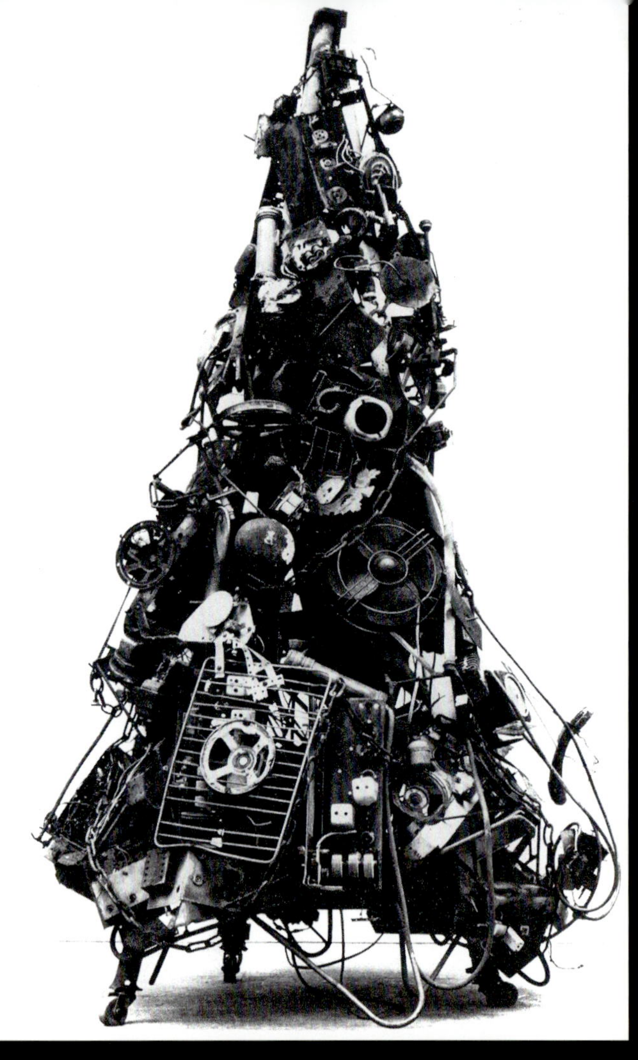

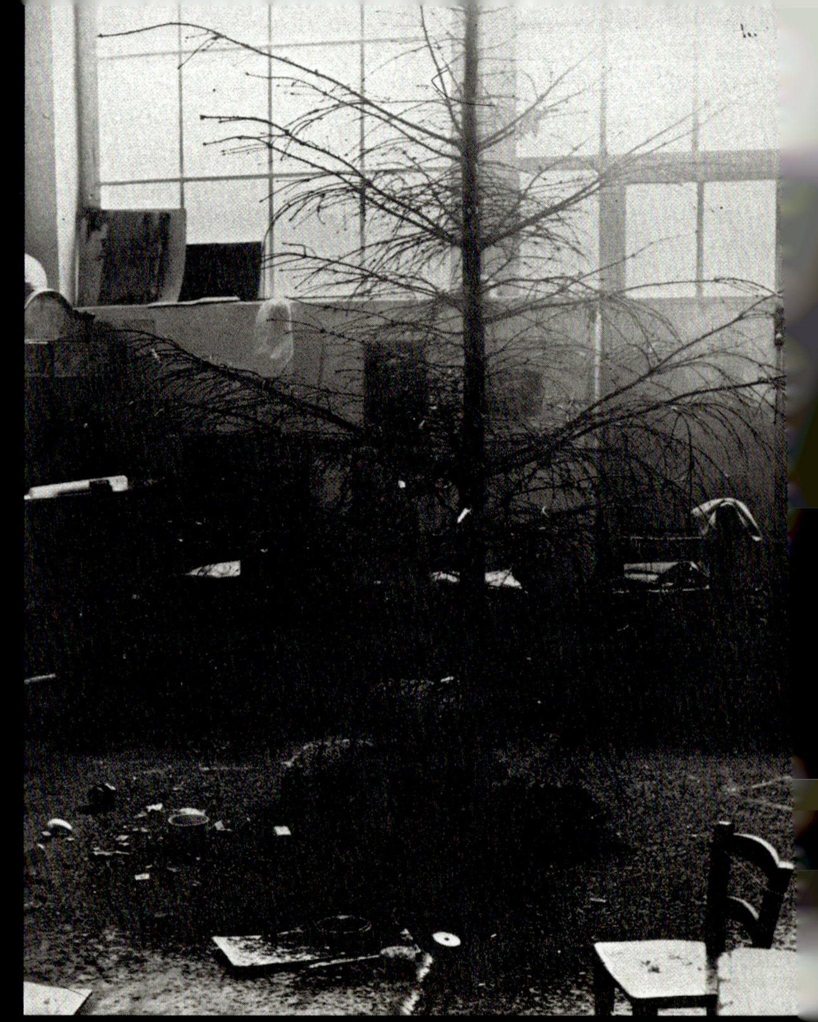

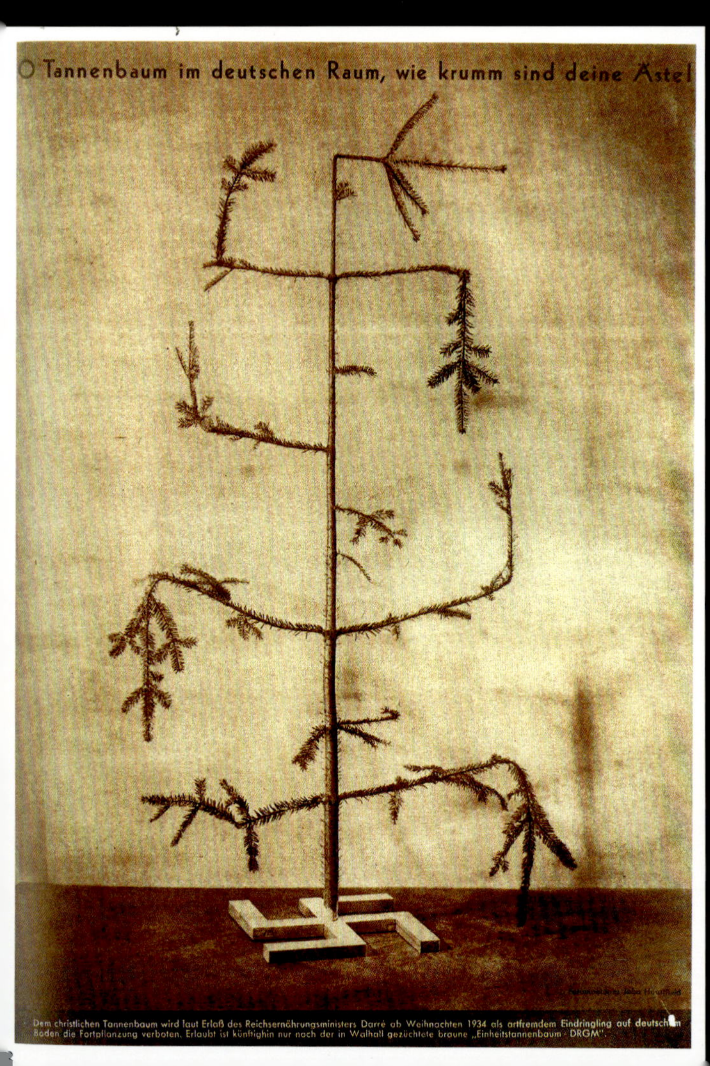
O Tannenbaum im deutschen Raum, wie krumm sind deine Äste!
Dem christlichen Tannenbaum wird laut Erlaß des Reichsernährungsministers Darré ab Weihnachten 1934 als artfremdem Eindringling auf deutsch m Boden die Fortpflanzung verboten. Erlaubt ist künftighin nur noch der in Walhall gezüchtete braune „Einheitstannenbaum - DRGM".

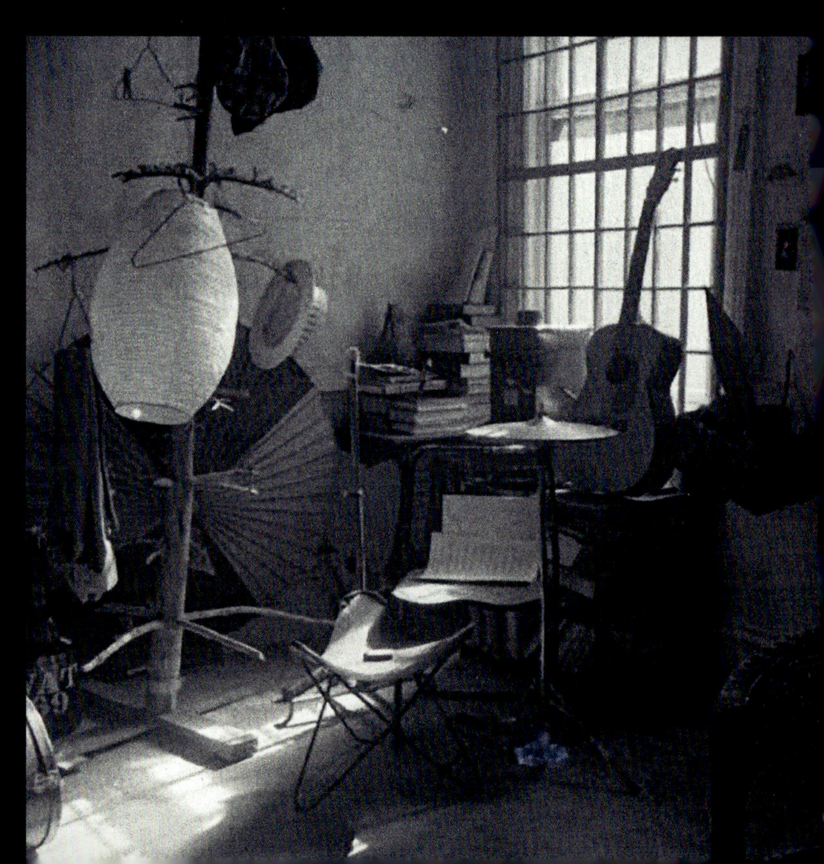

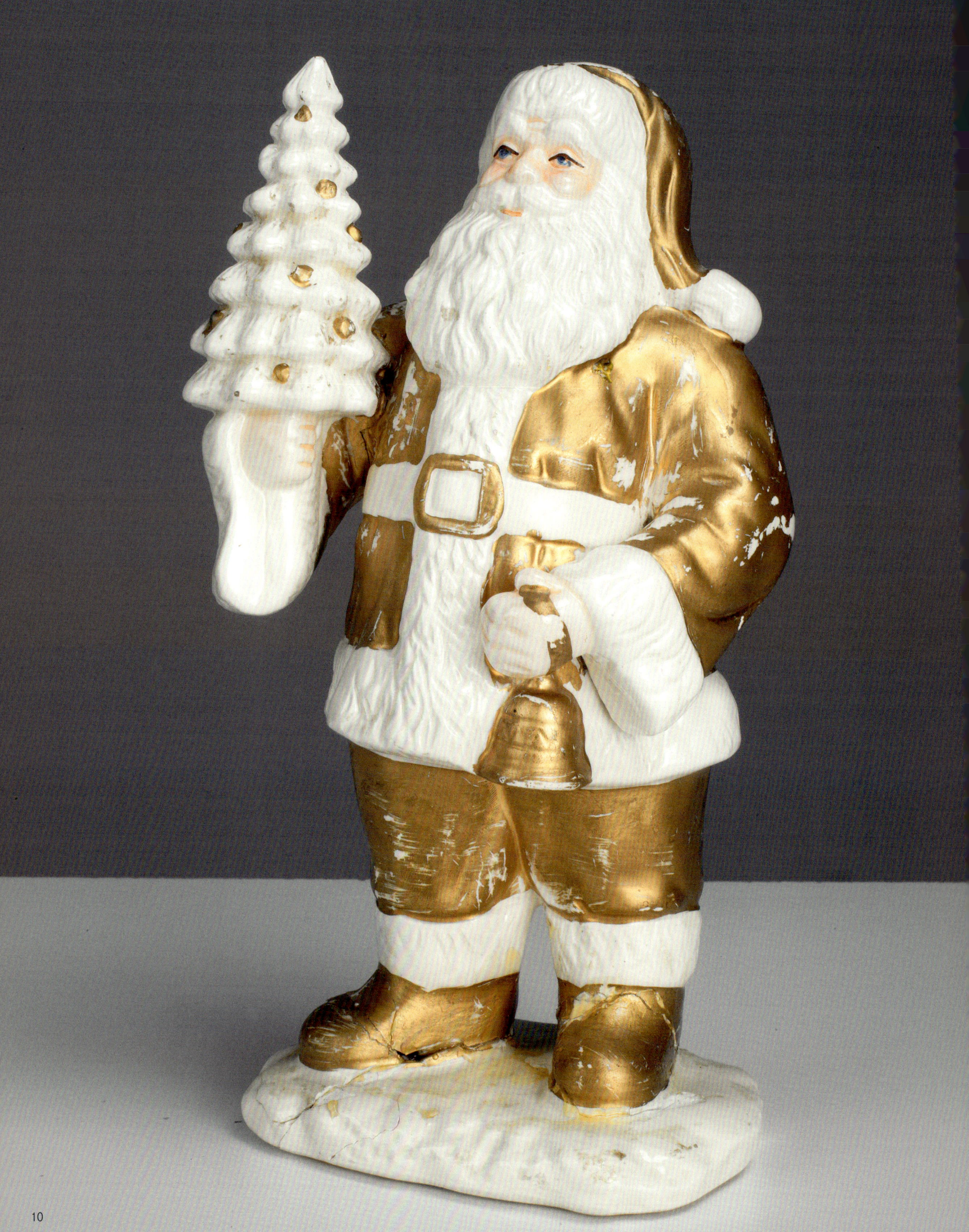

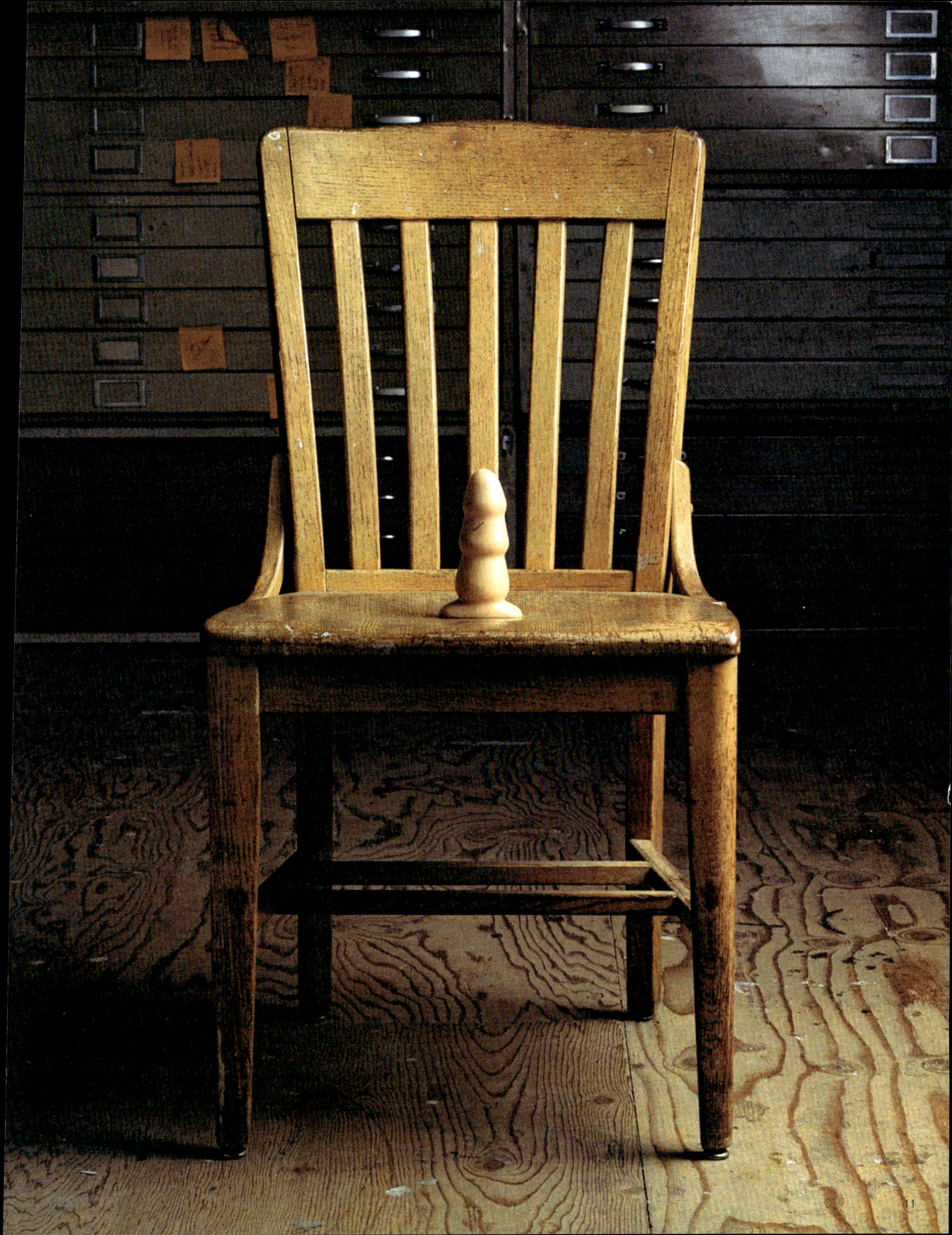

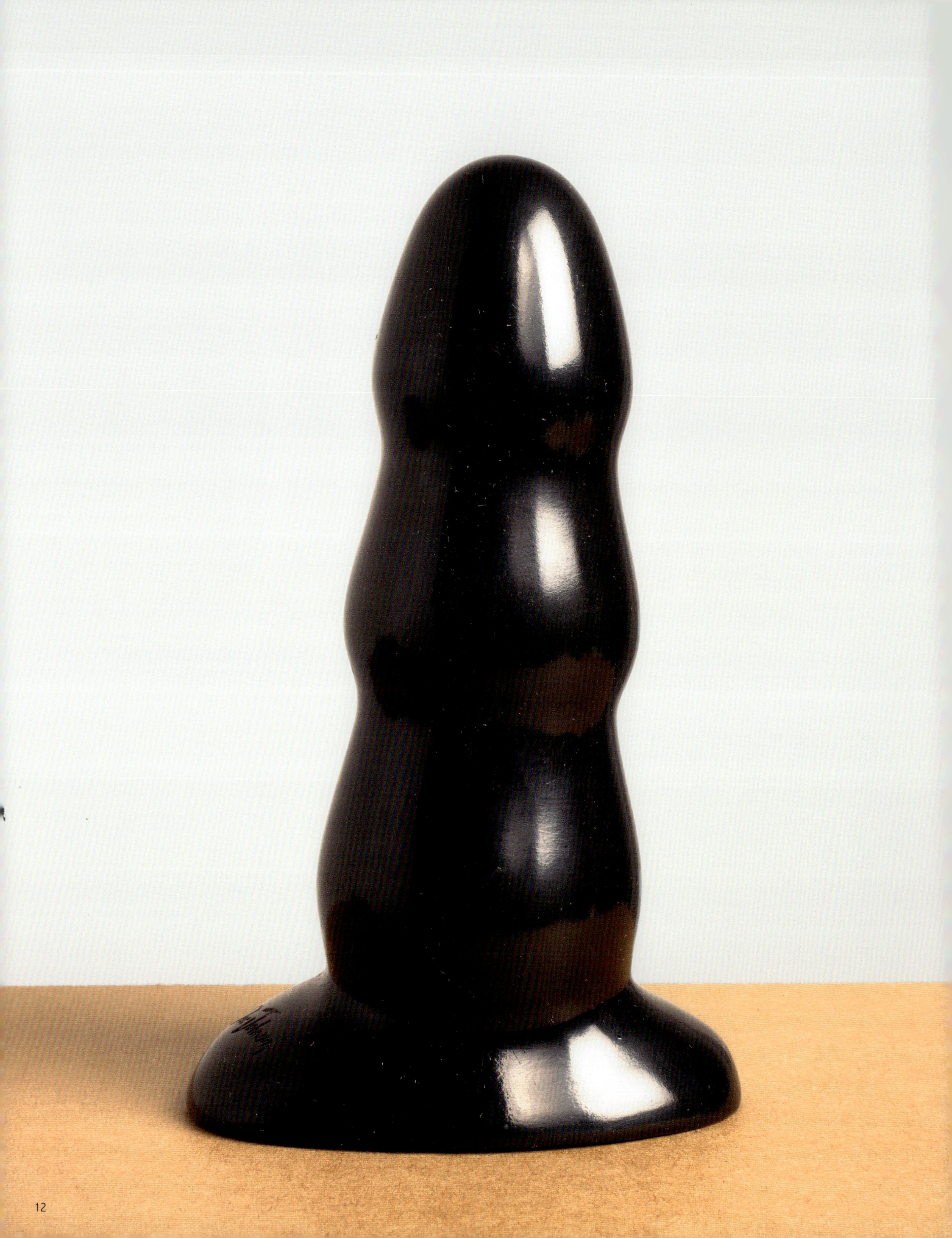

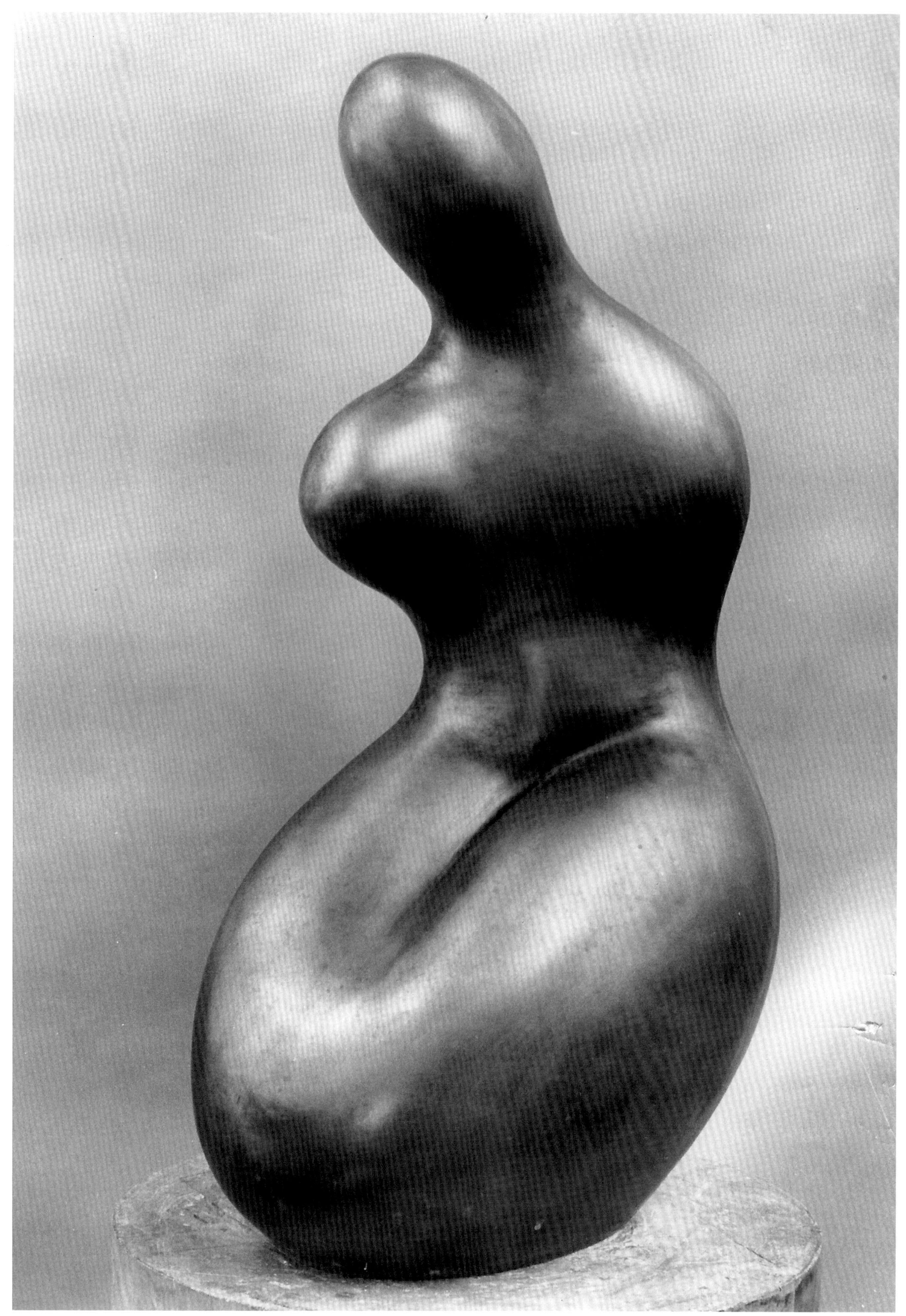

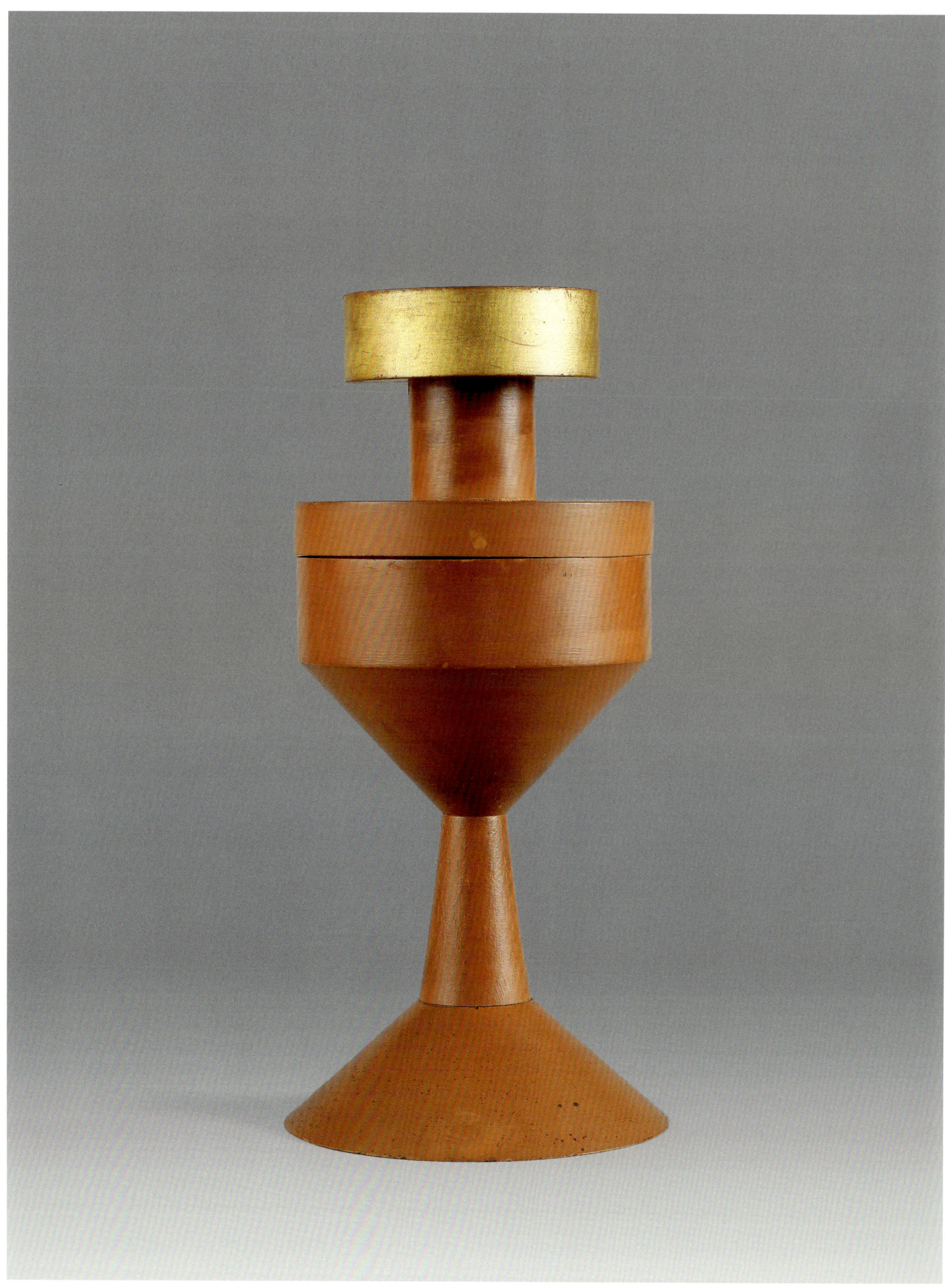

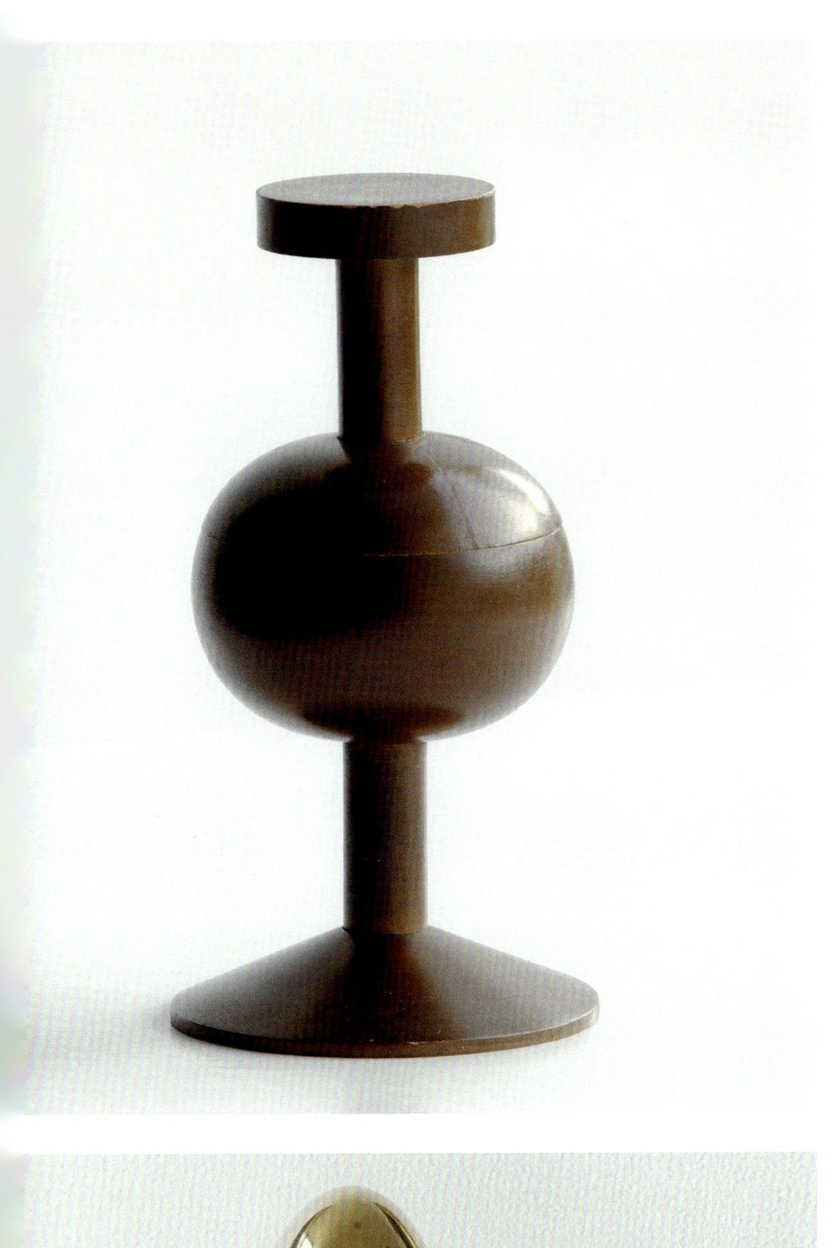
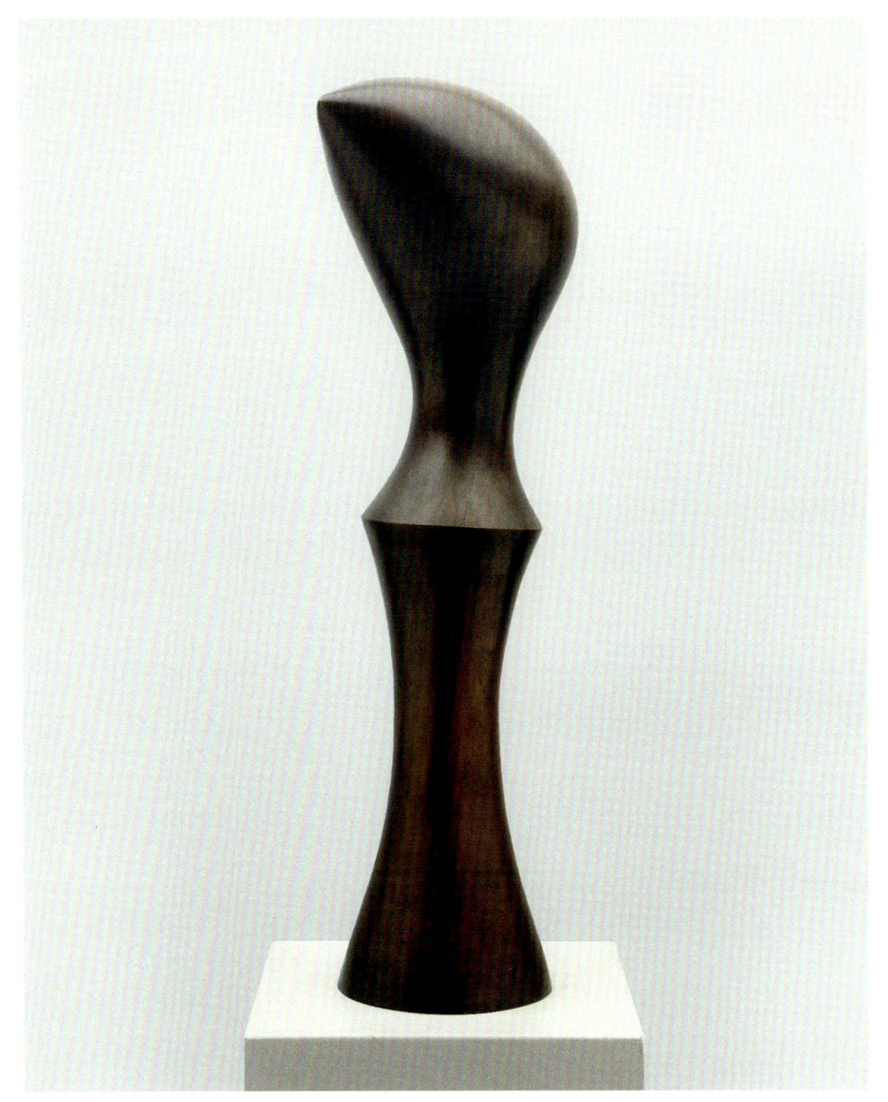
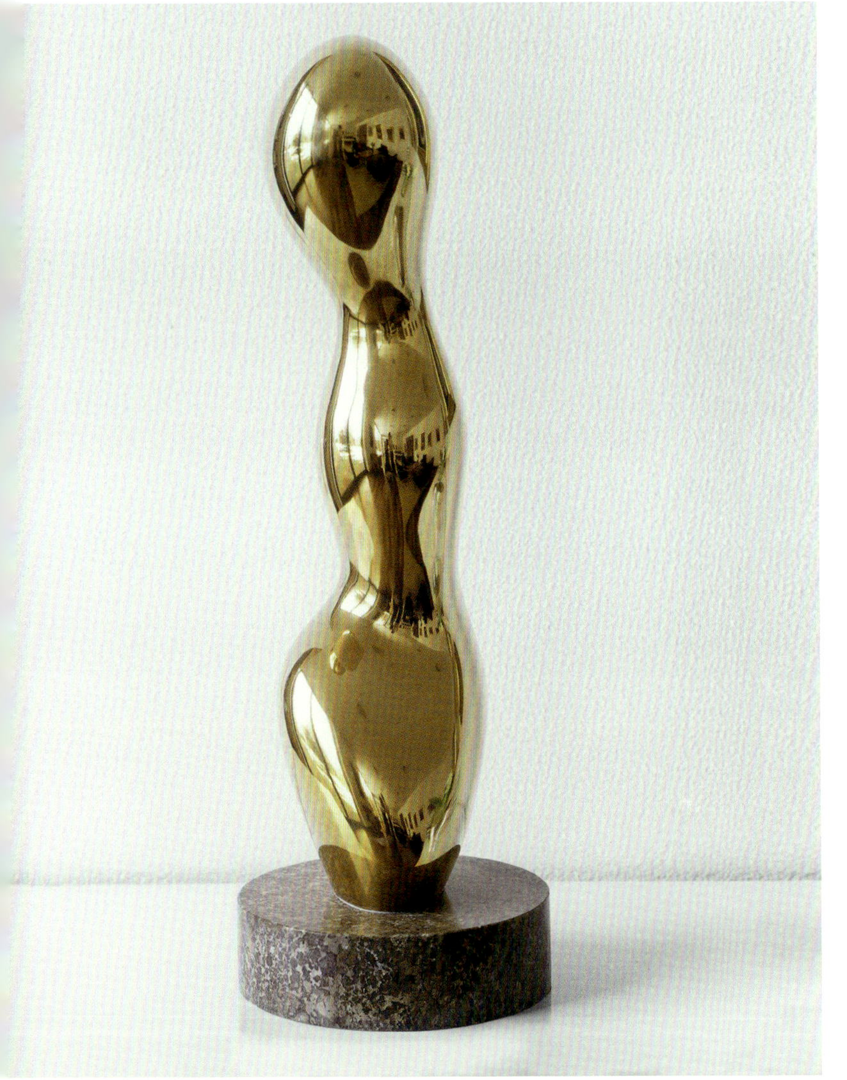
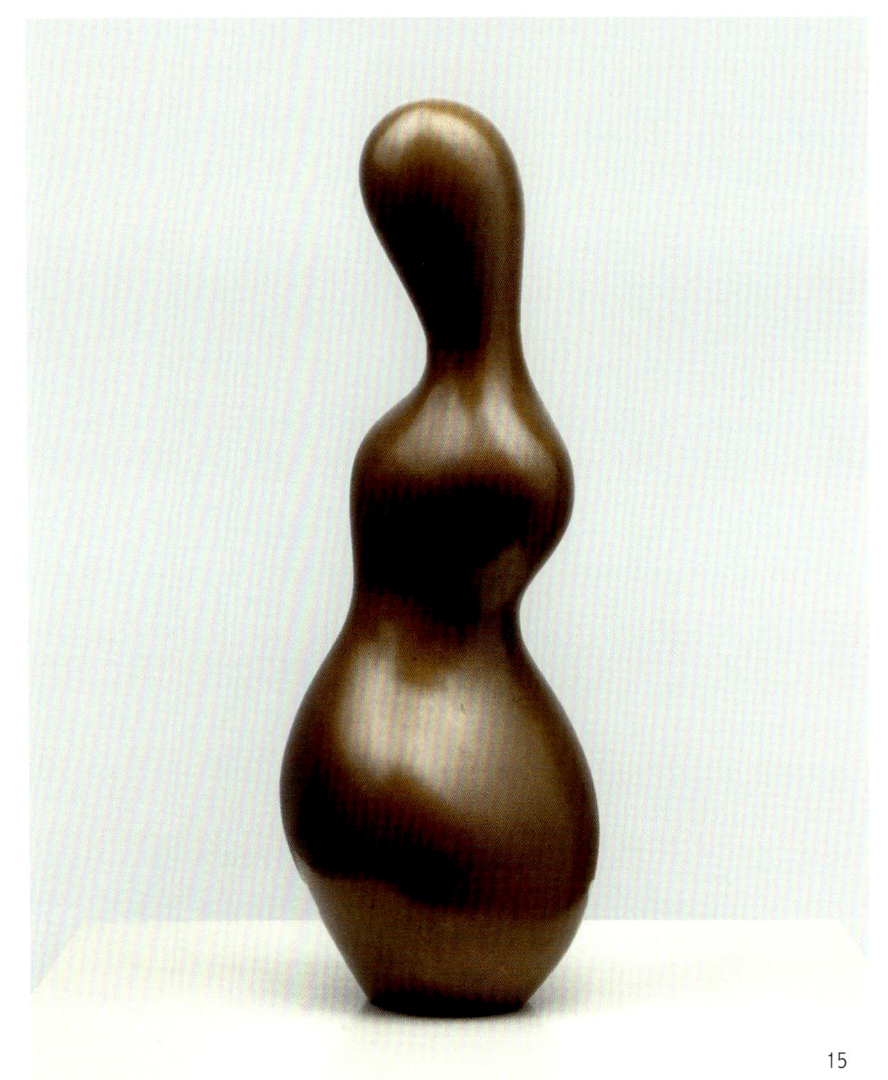

Chocolate
Factory
Chocolate
Sublimation

Santa Claus patriarch Christmas tree tree root Trio Trio Trio plug
correct the anal sexual content content content pretend
pretense productions pinner technology spinner
organization of the body production delirium in itself refers to other
parts of the body being sublimated do to his delusion lose diluted the
architecture the production humiliated performance intense
preoccupation with the fixation rest arrested movement his scenes
are frozen as though the show copy it I want to show you another
portrait of me one that I painted myself you shall copy the painting
it suggest both the sternness of the order and the reflection of the
mirror photographed effect of the displacement onto the anal region of
the function the round hole access in and out to of the interior body
and interior to enter her and value of other parts of the body
sublimation chocolate we said in an earlier chapter in the search for
the outside world outside of the architecture use it on the outside of
you nursing from she from her face on the outside of the house her her
skull school her architecture architect and search and search in the
outside world for the lost body of childhood but the body that was
lost was already the chocolate figurine an allusion the plug
production as plug befuddled body befuddled by the confusion caused by
the fantasy desire substitute desire substitute becoming father of
oneself endless production one figurine figuring out a time labor
production paid labor and therefore for example abusing the feces the
shit the value of the penis or child child's penis shit shit as penis
thus if the money complex is derived from the Smith money paid
complexes derived from an anal complex the anal complex this to the
terminology production technology endless production pretenses media
and image pretense image unification particular regions of the
totality of the architecture of the body the architecture was in
architecture for media architecture as reflection of cultural value
notions of opulent perfection containing the culture of the fake
containing production fixation products fixation anal fixation
chocolate syrup feces route resistant occupation to occupy the
building time period mirror reflection this architecture being on the
outside you being on the outside of the body the plug plug is for the
to go up round hole one enters through sits on the fingering sculpture
the plug one architecture within another fantasy architecture as
division divider derived money from the infantile impulse to play with
shit she sees sublimated by the impingement on this play impulse ship
shit supplemented by chocolate of a reproduction of feces play
sublimated which the development of upright posture money is the end
results which says after work has been said look attention the outside
of the architecture what's in the architecture inside the main body of
the childhood the body that was is lost

Paul McCarthy 2014

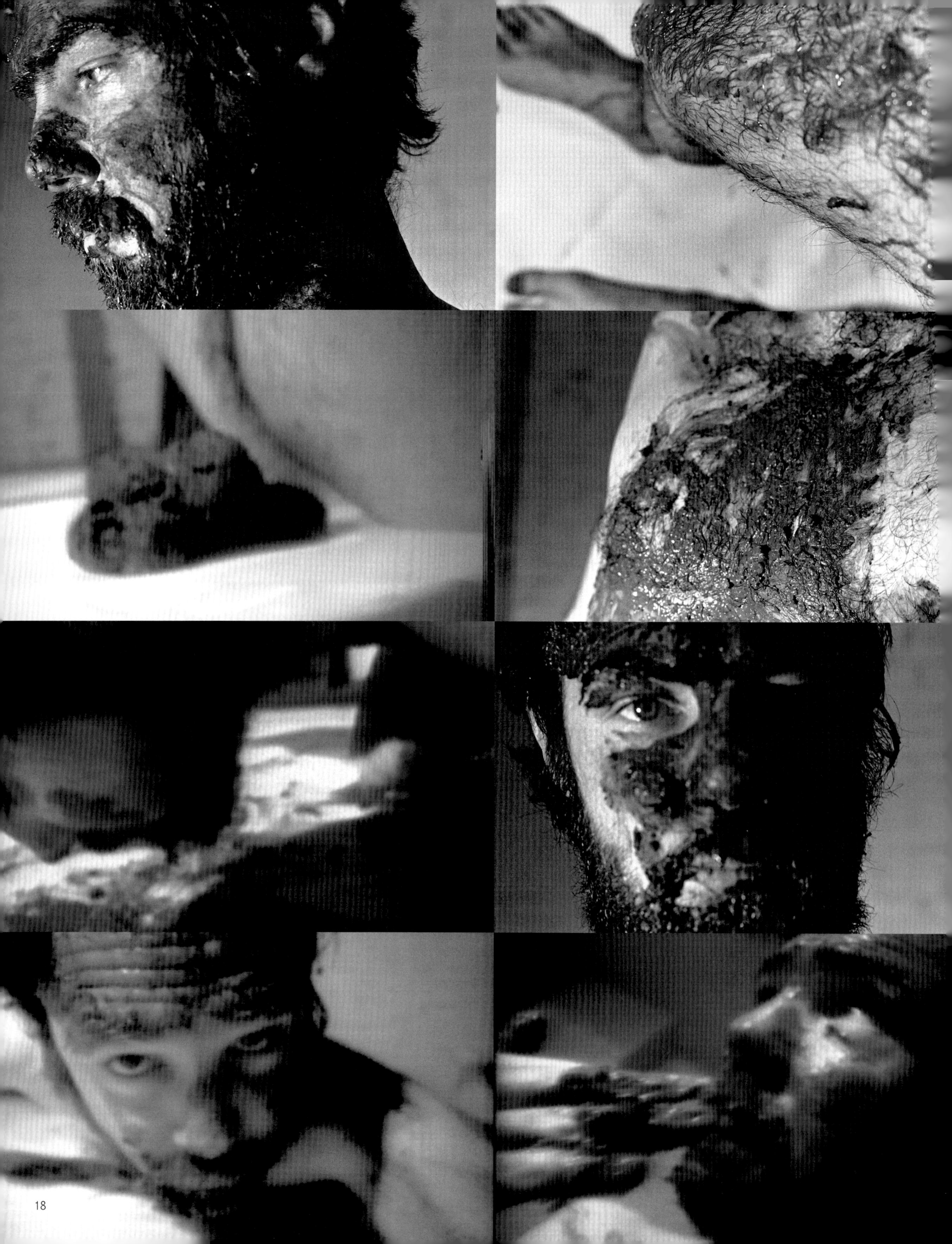

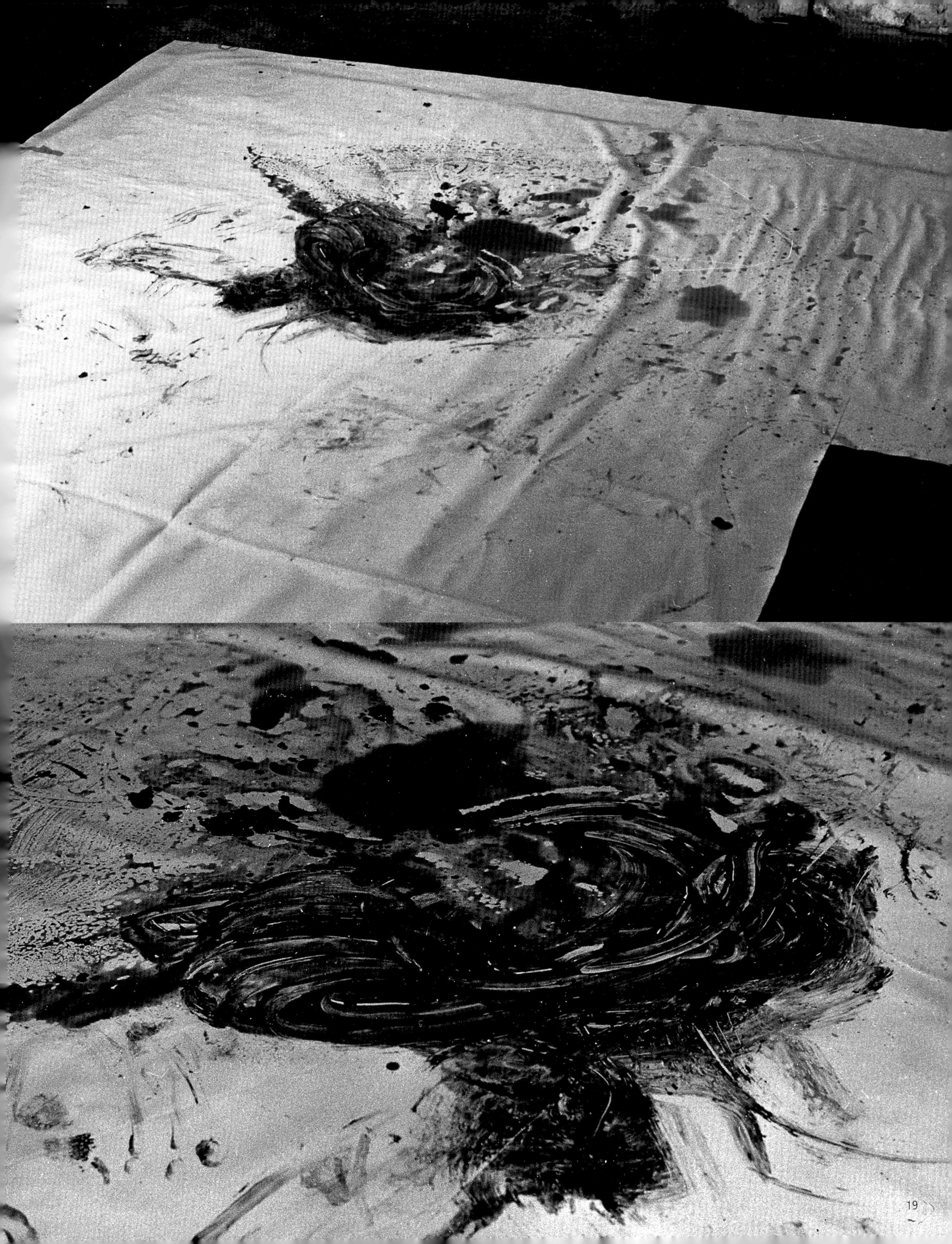

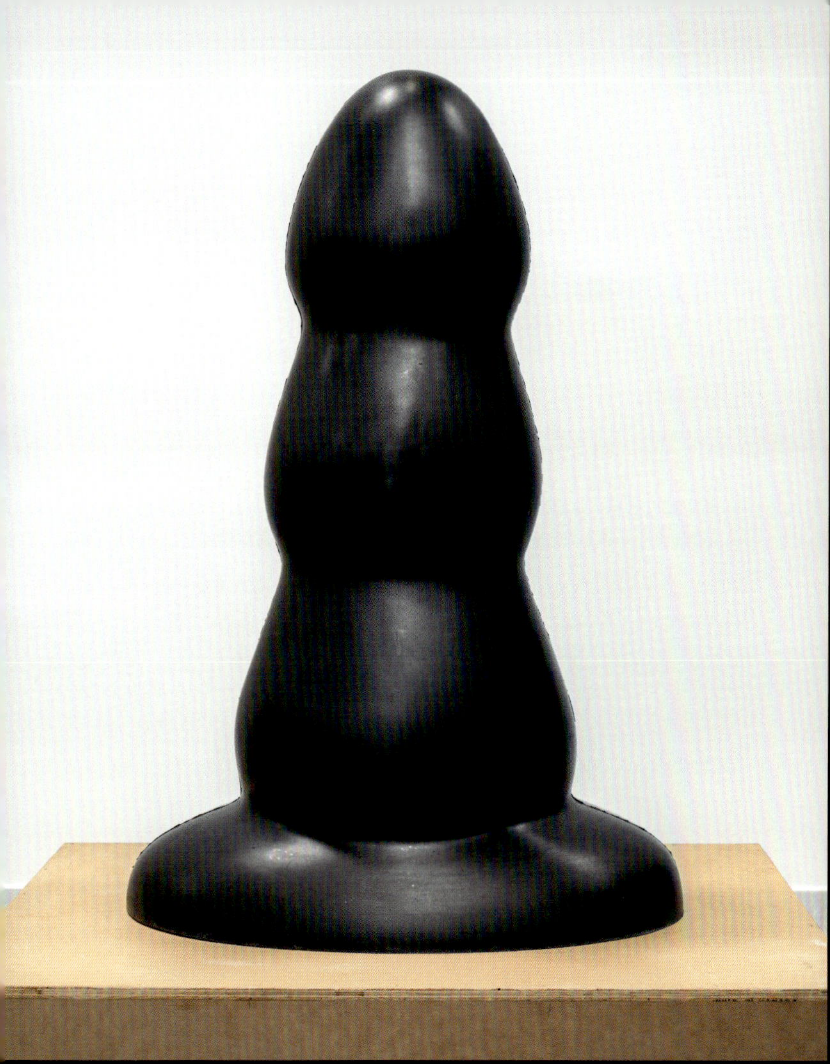

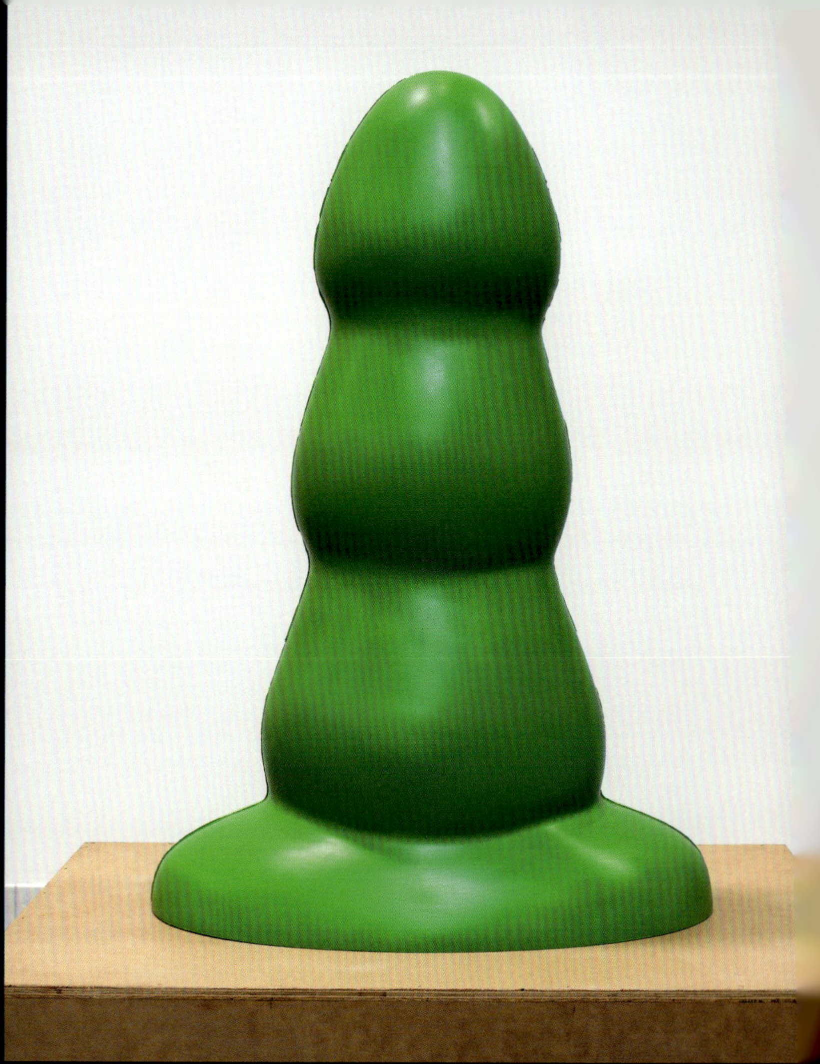

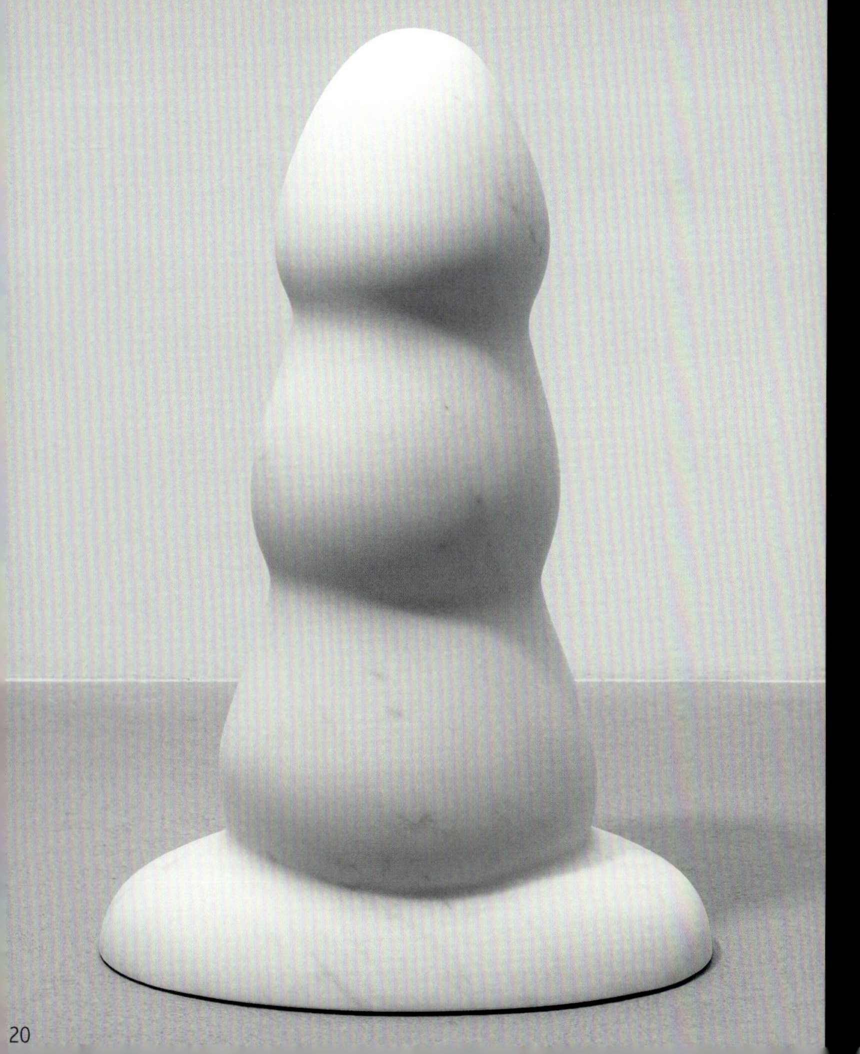

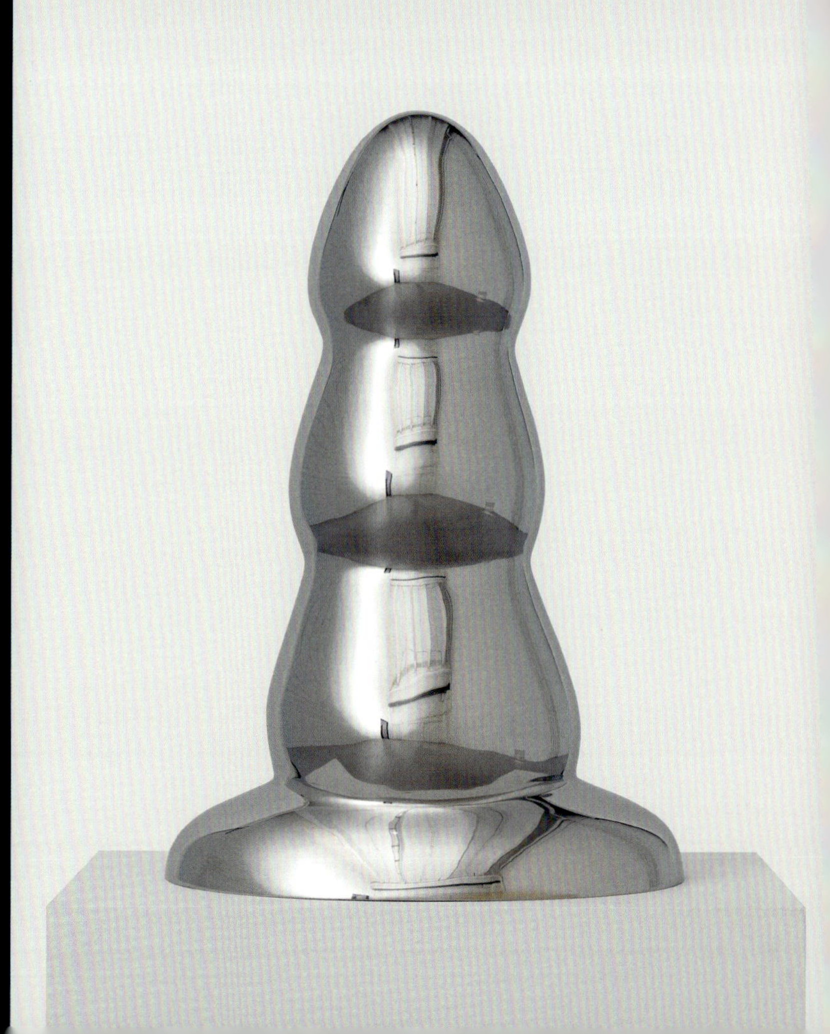

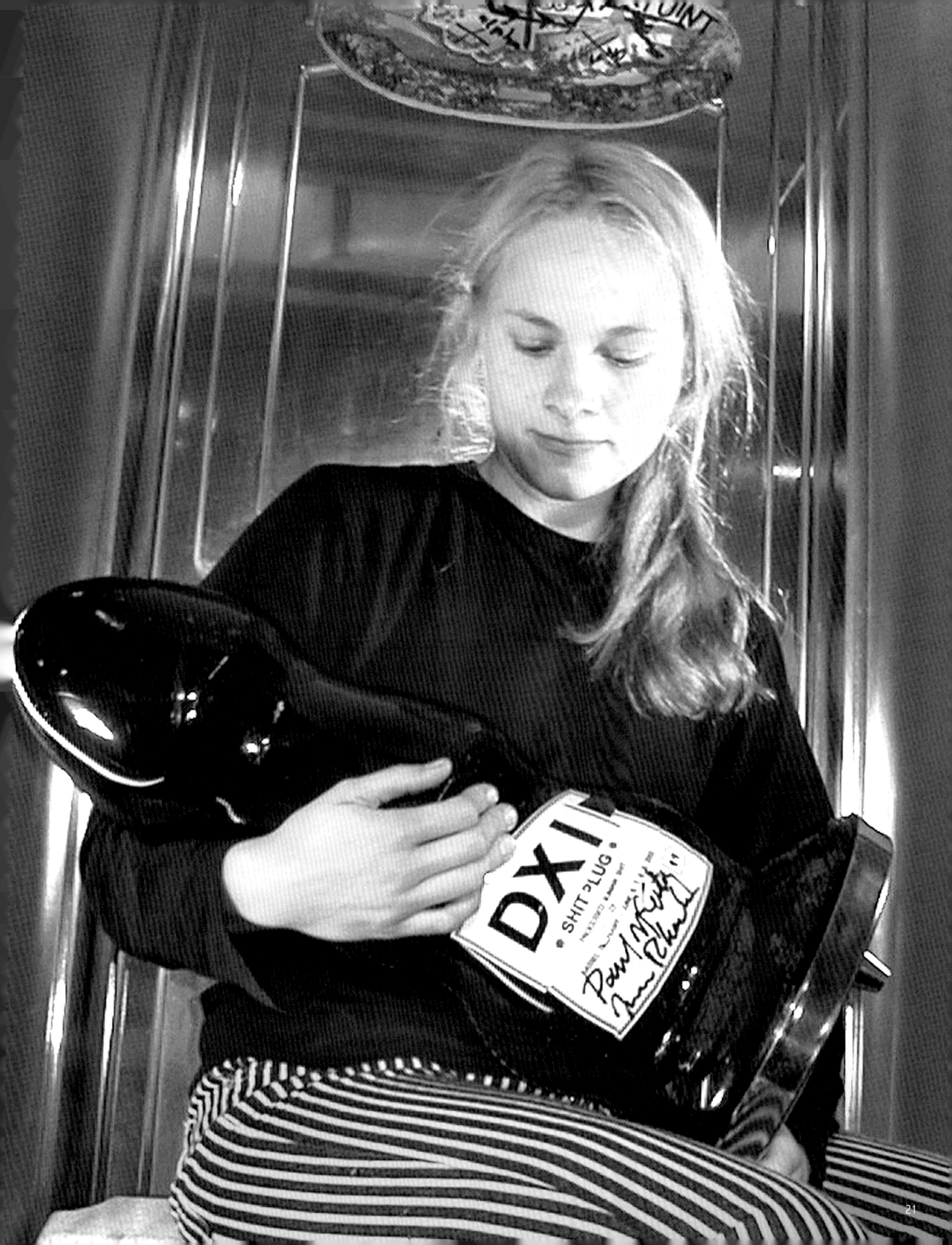
DX I
SHIT PLUG

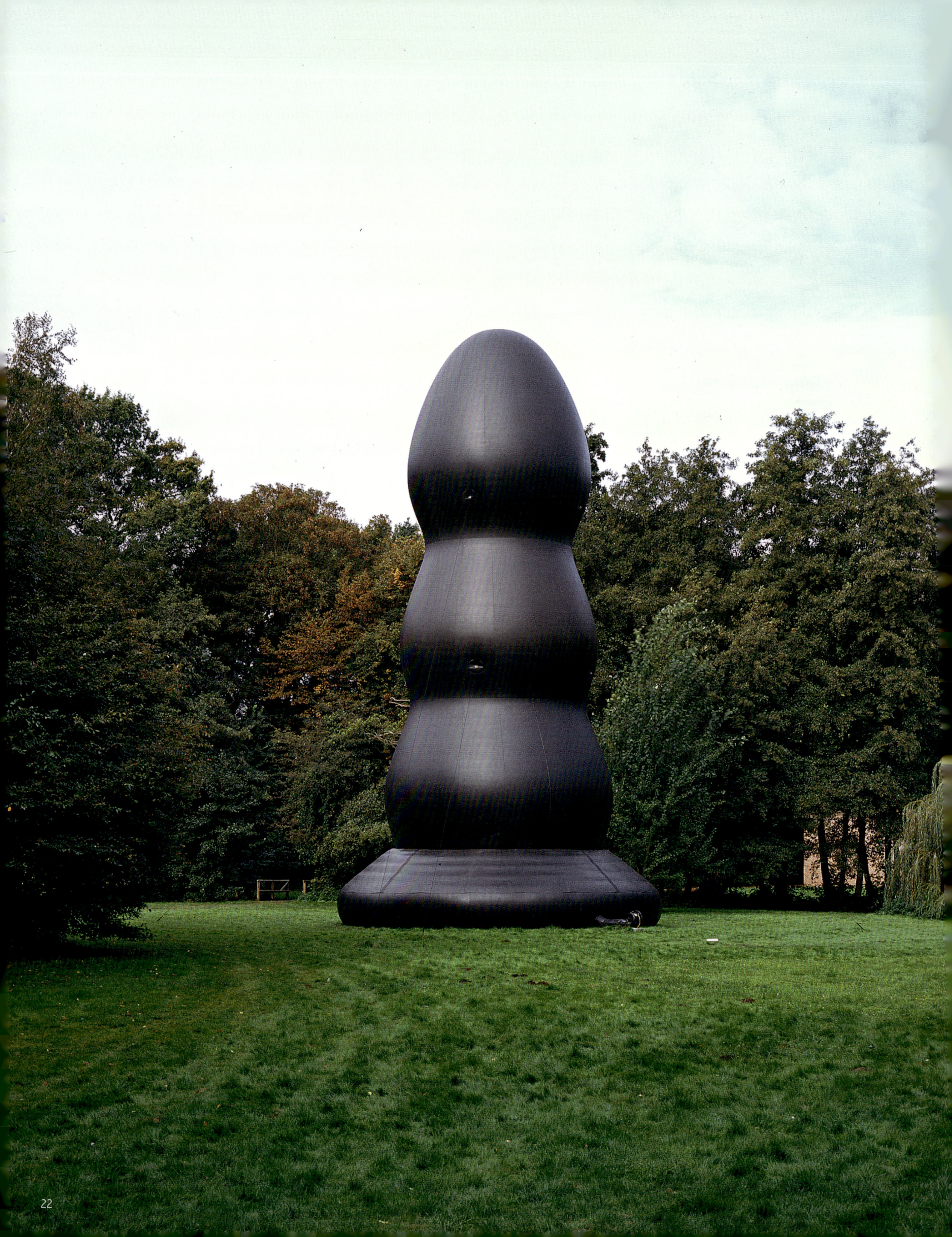

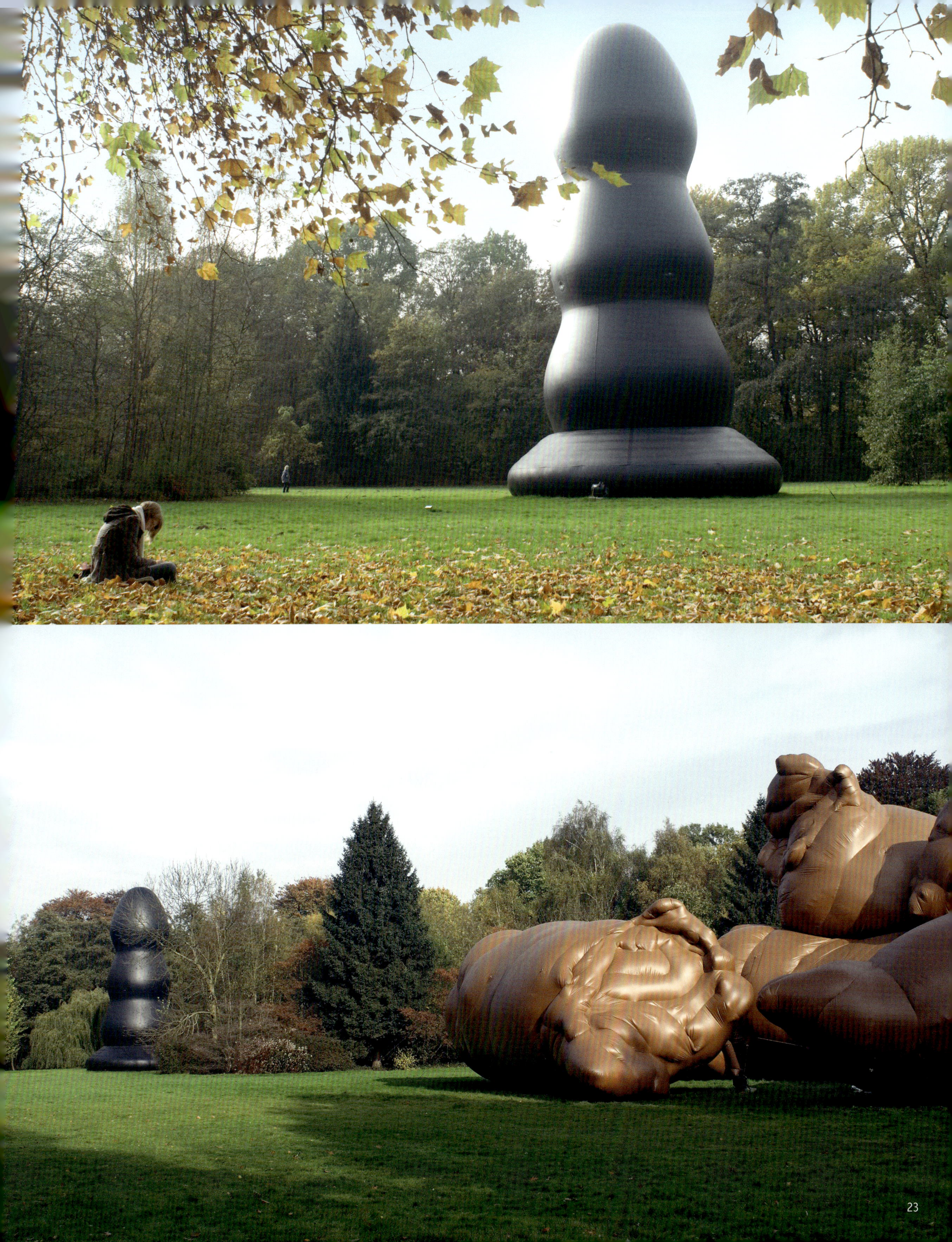

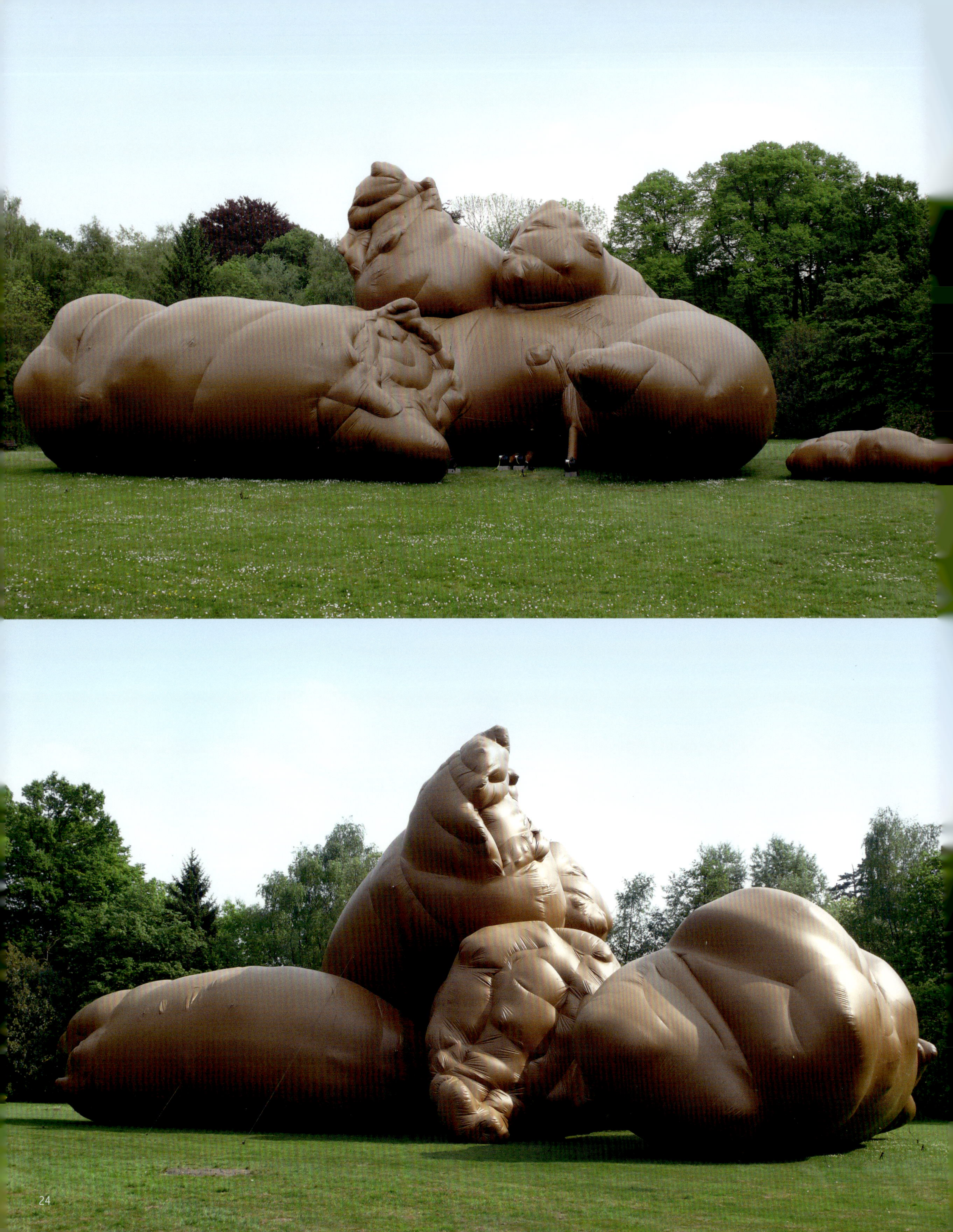

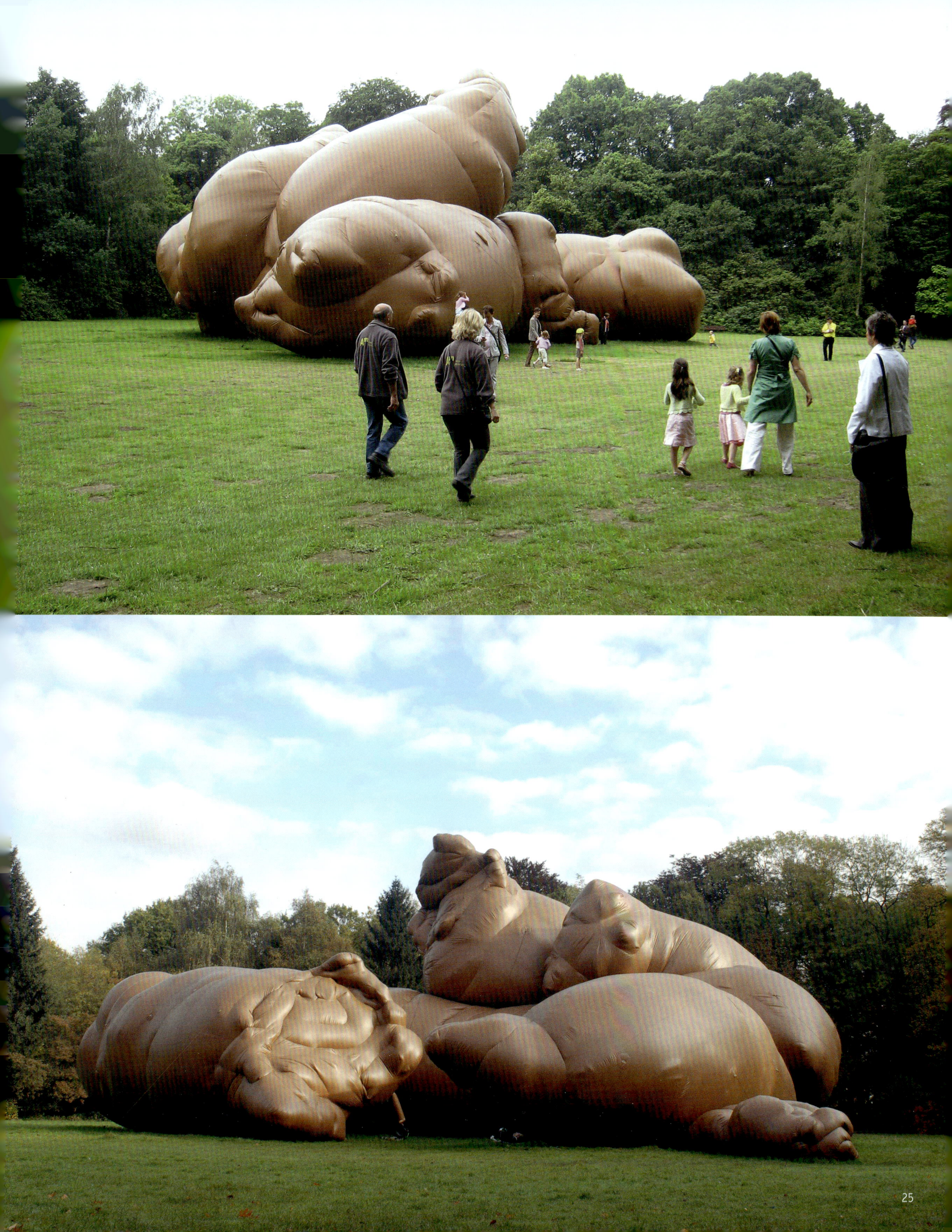

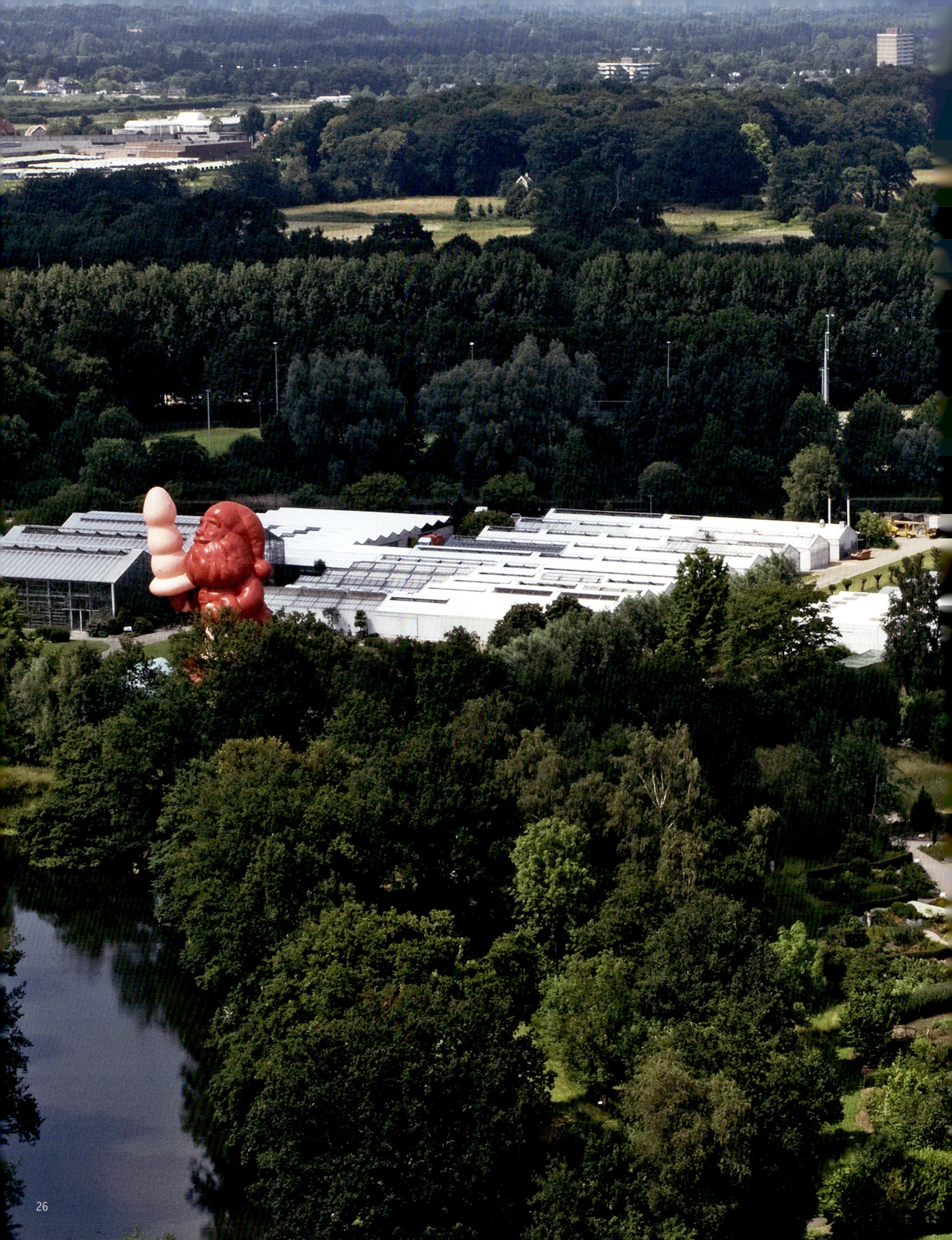

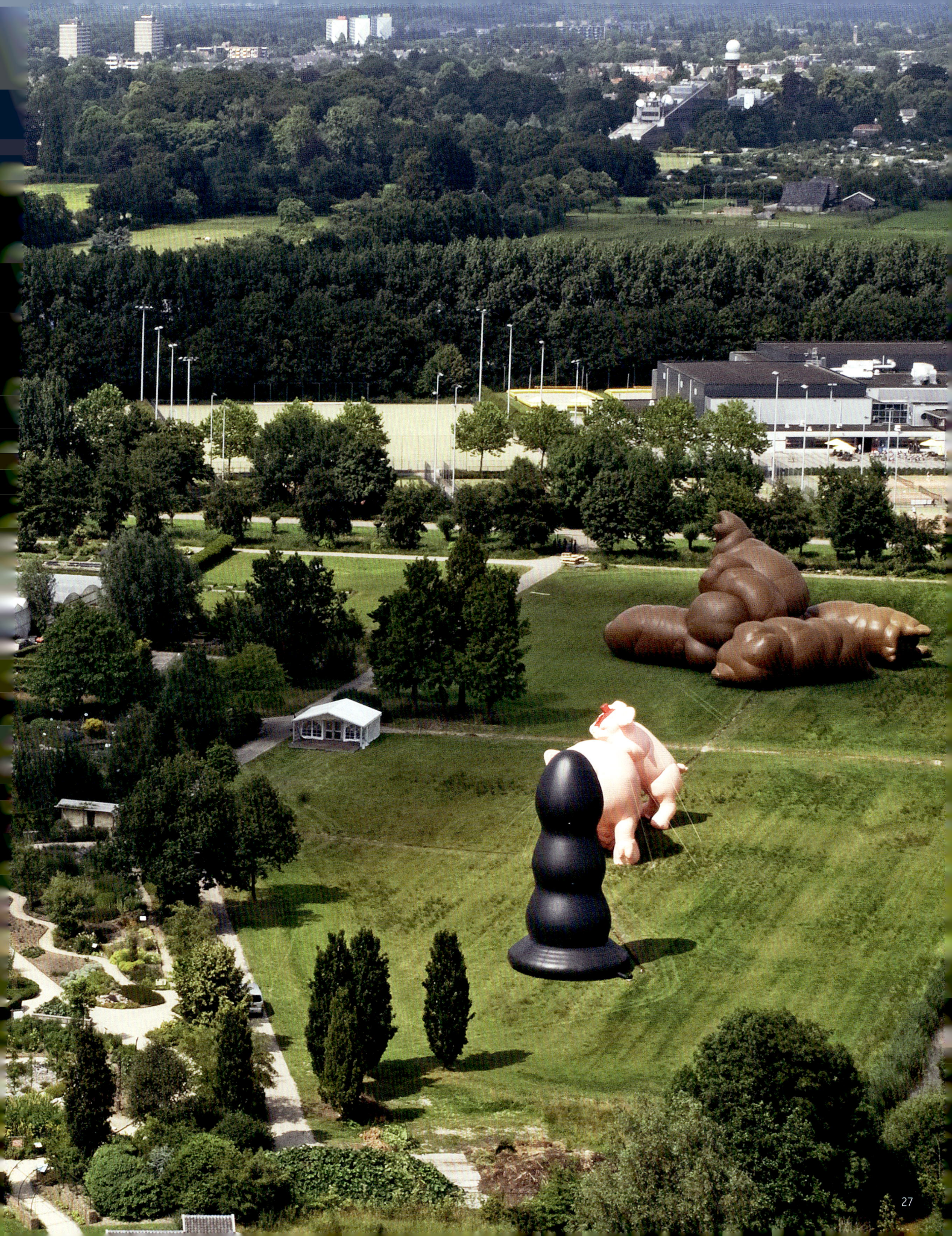

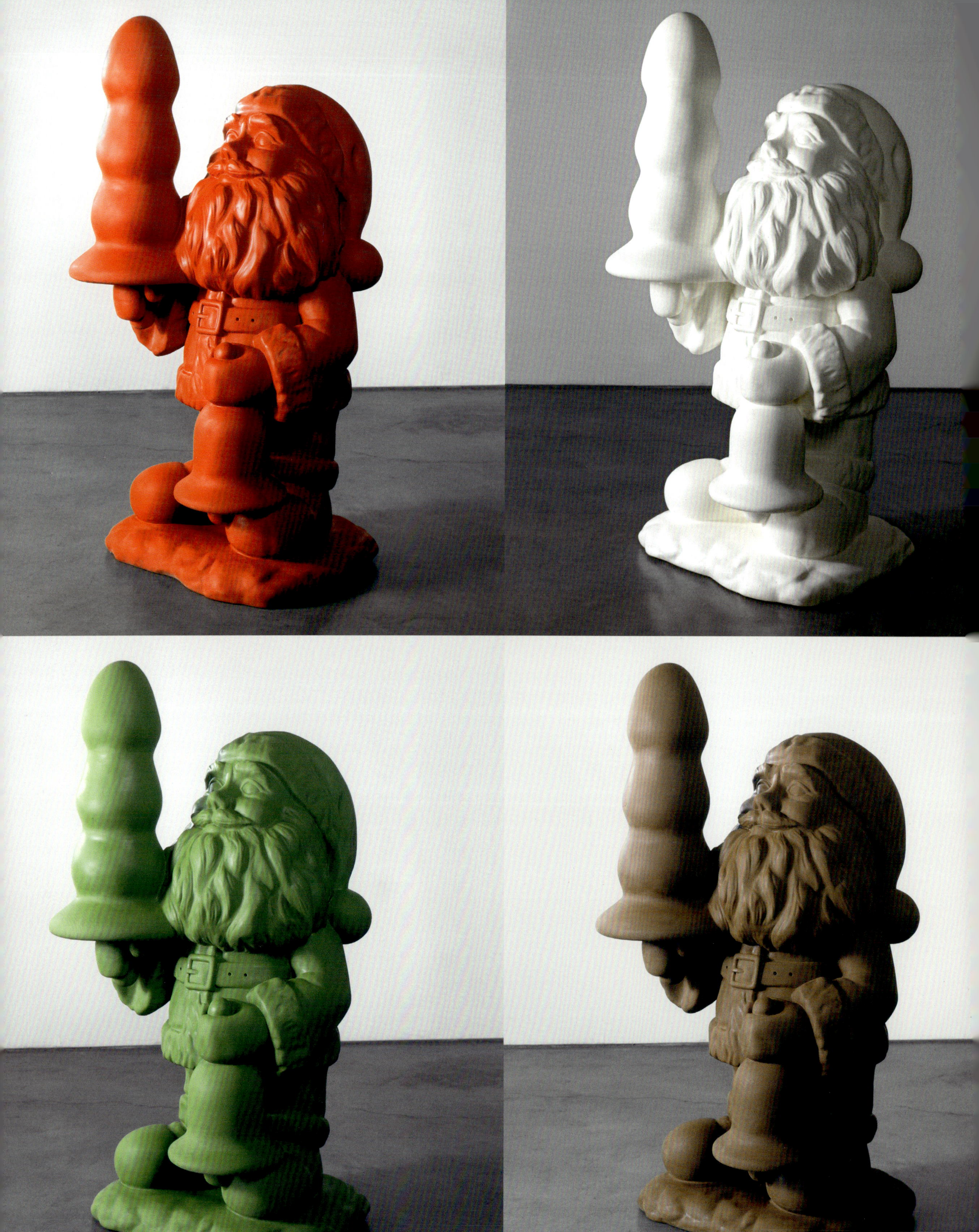

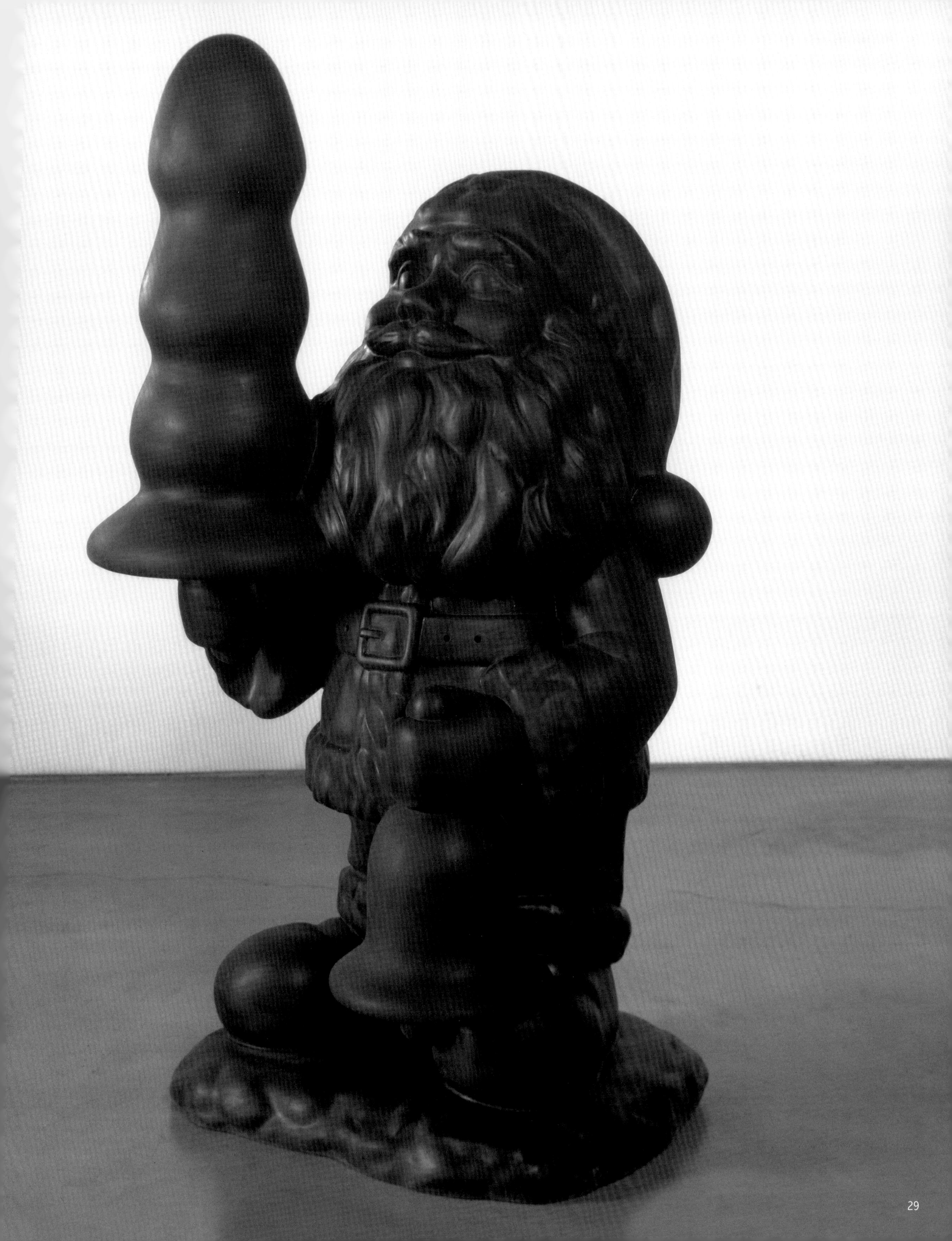

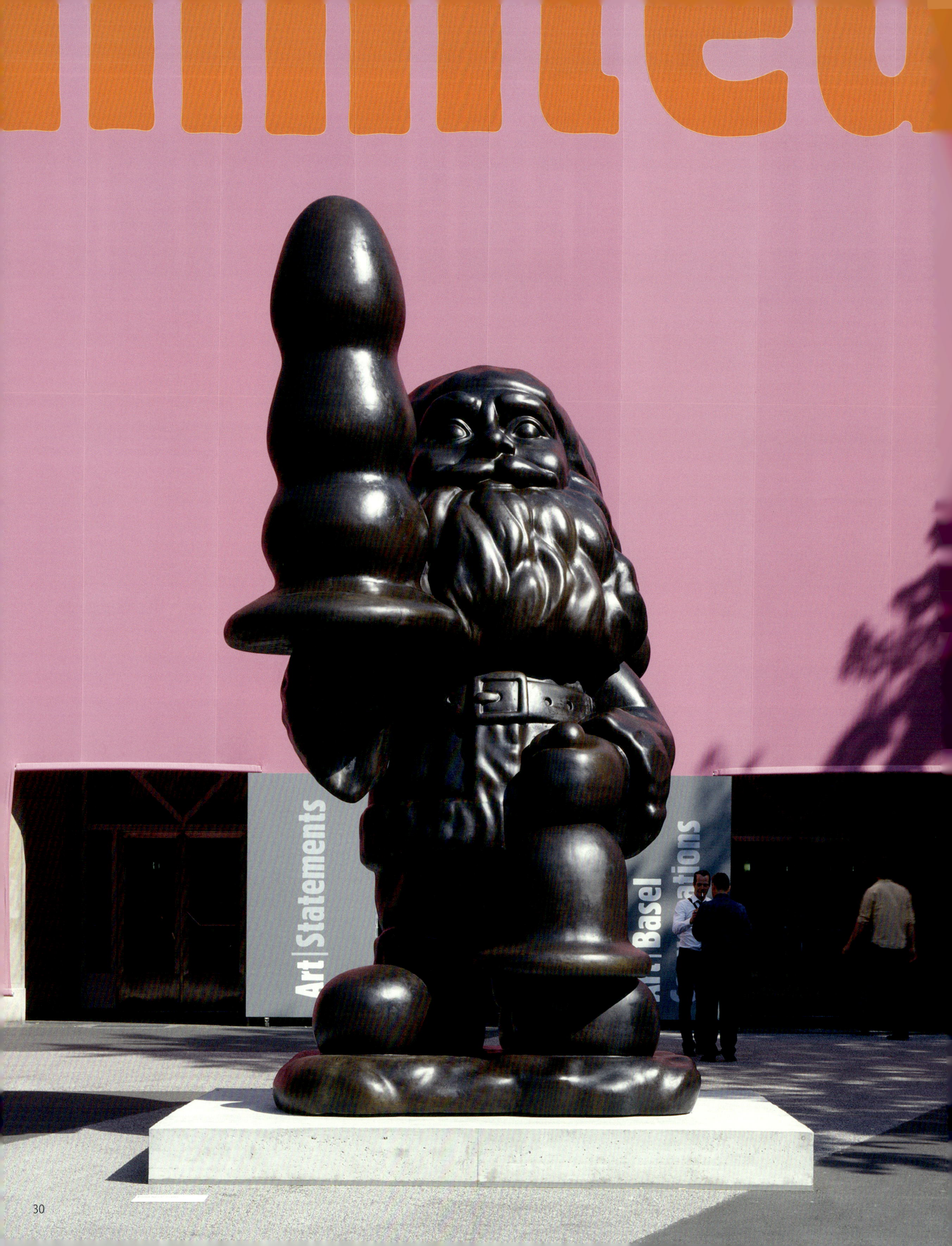
Art | Statements
Art | Basel

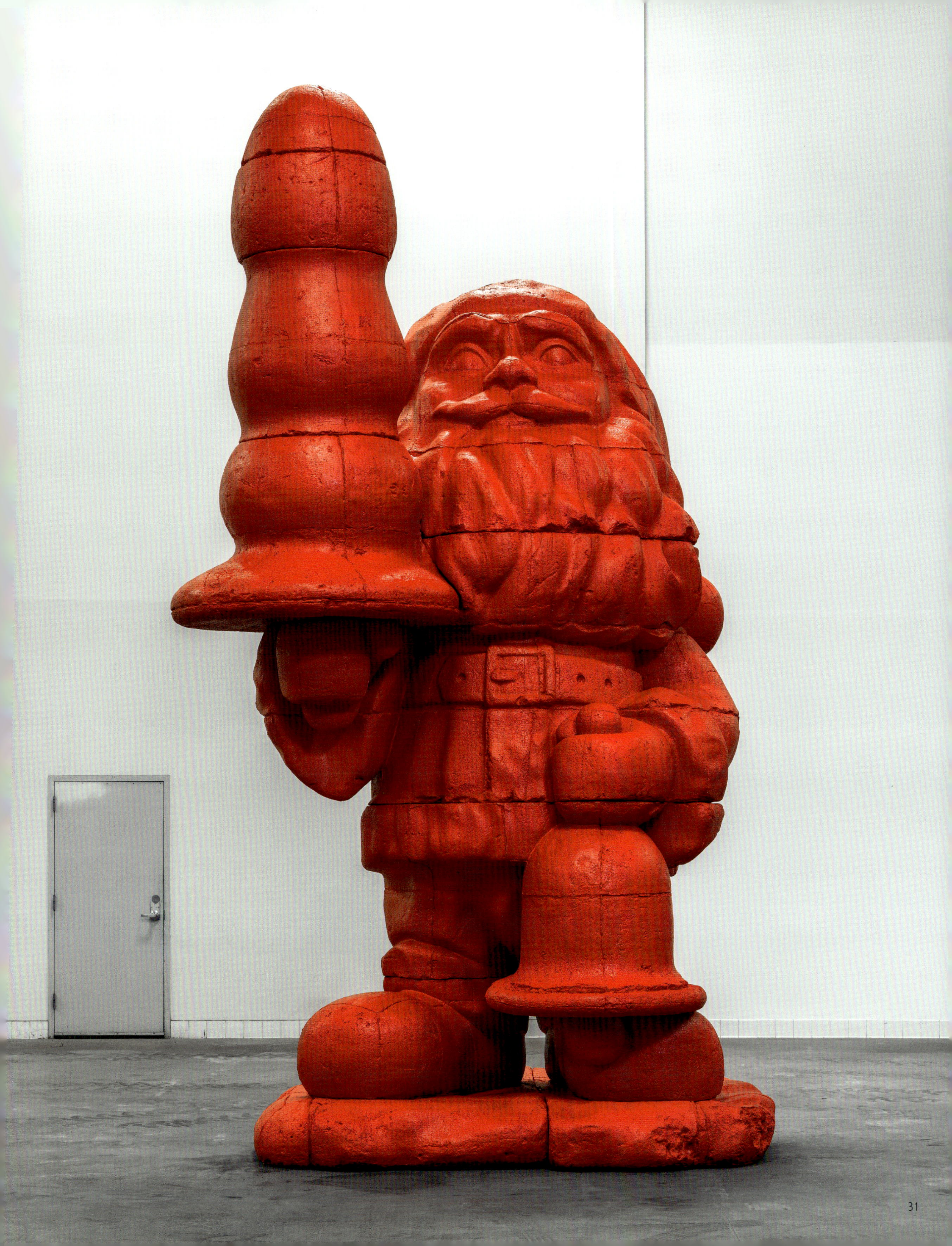

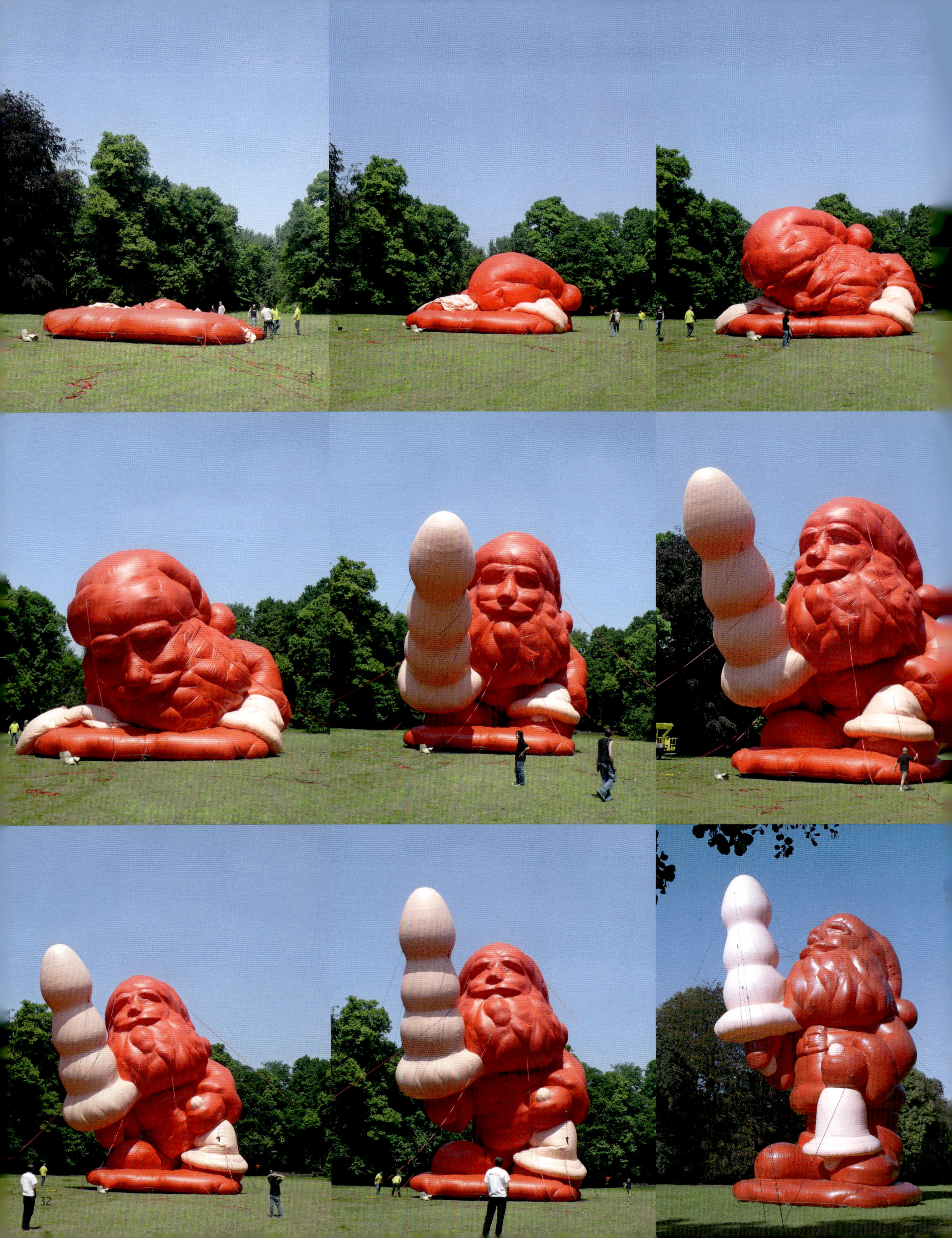

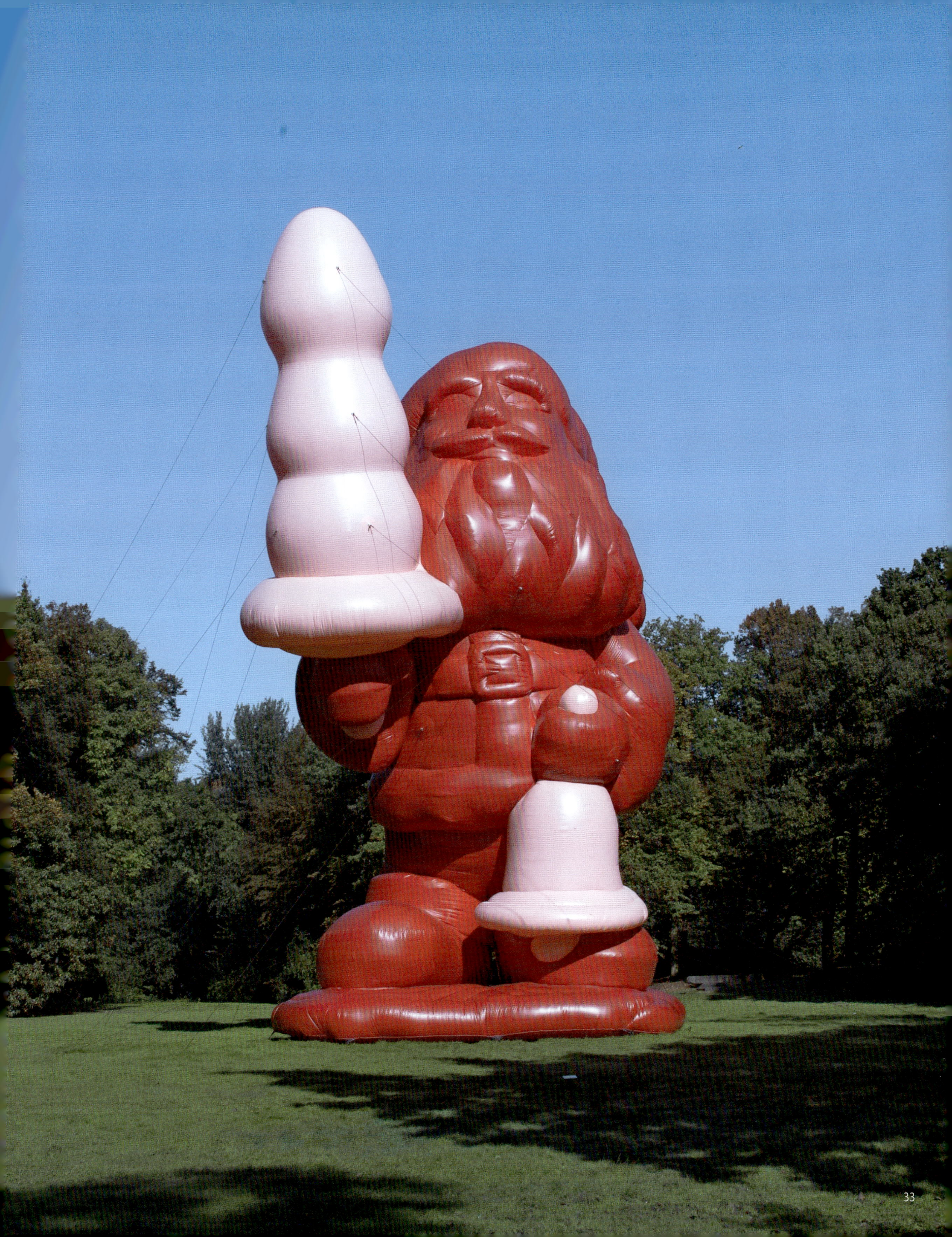

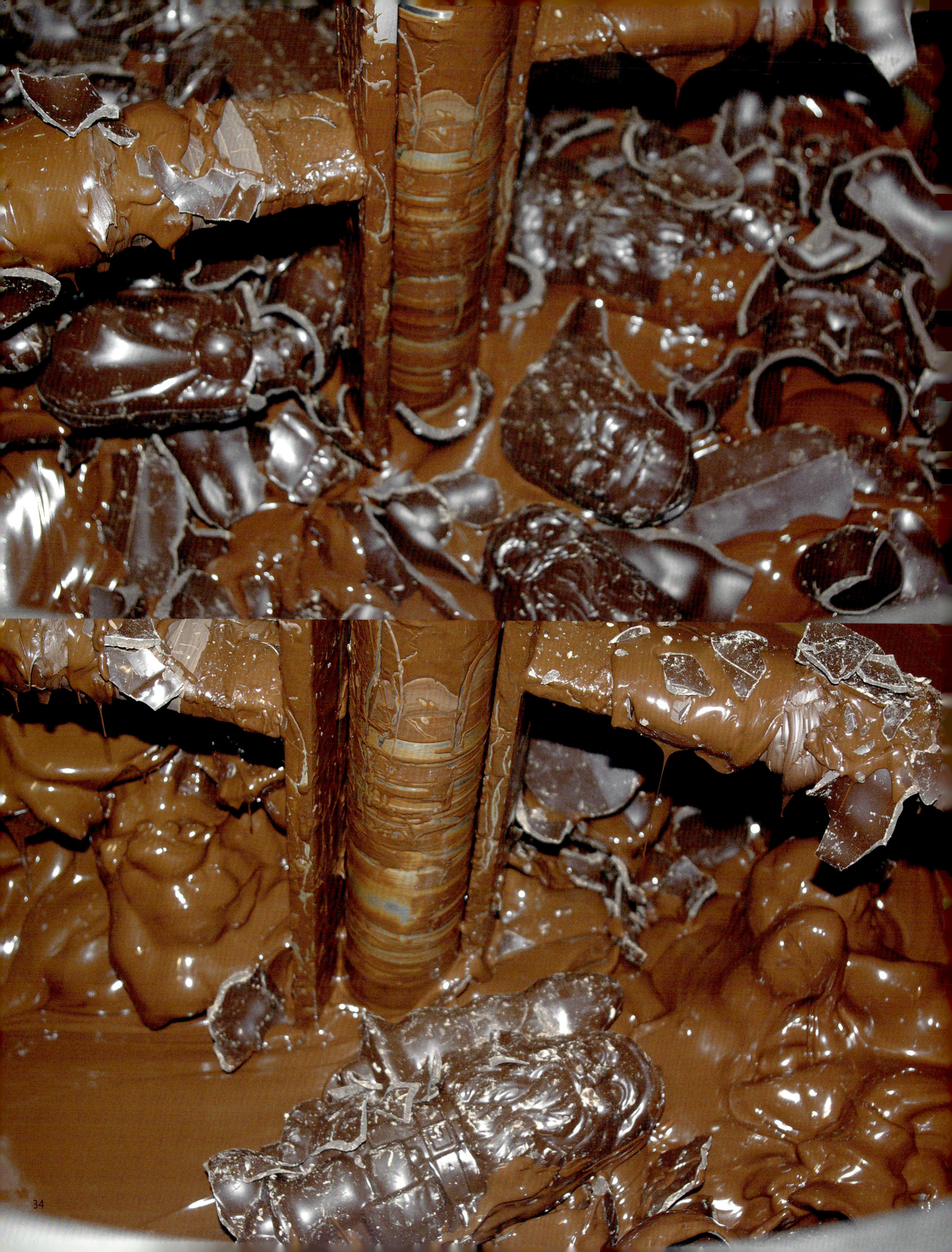

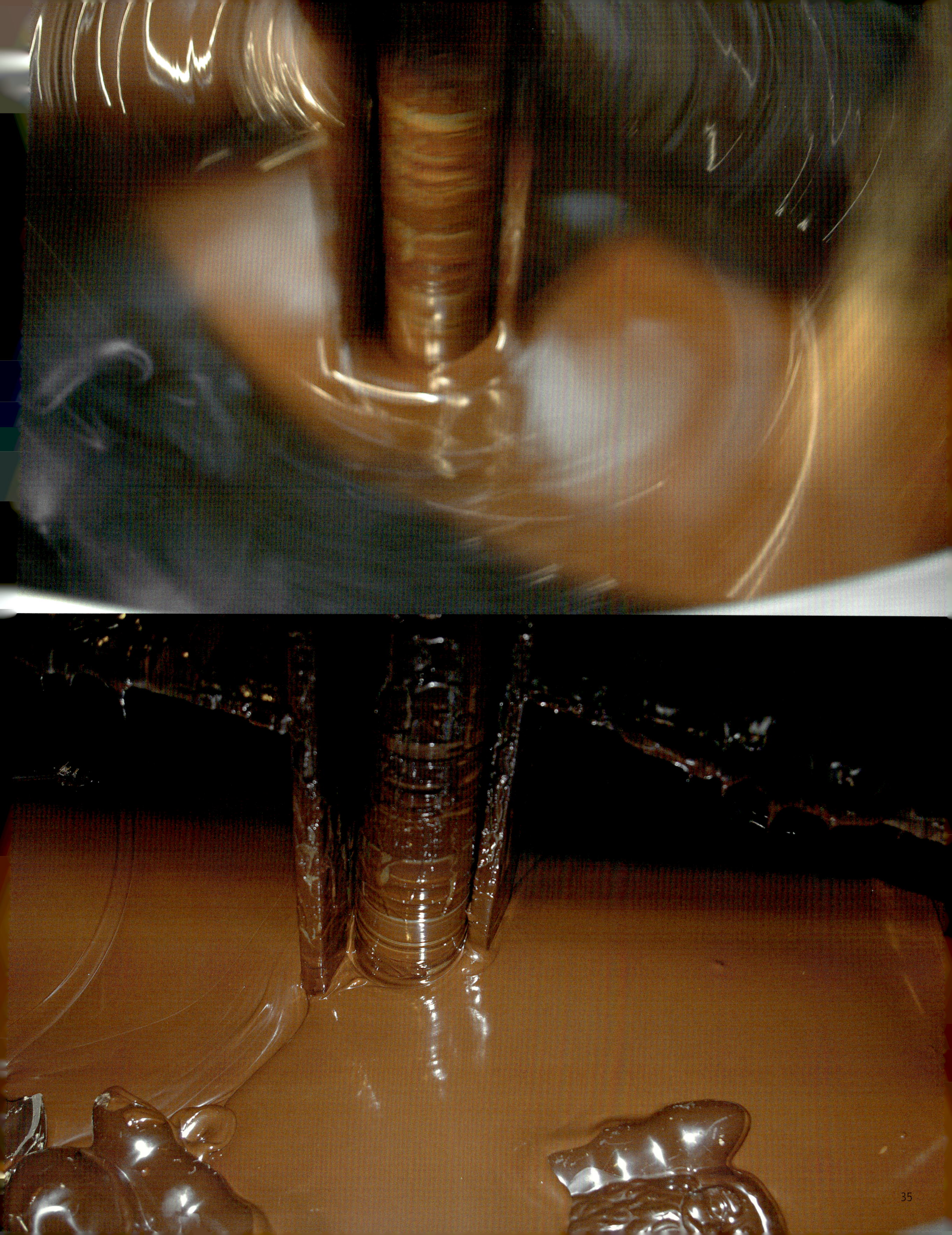

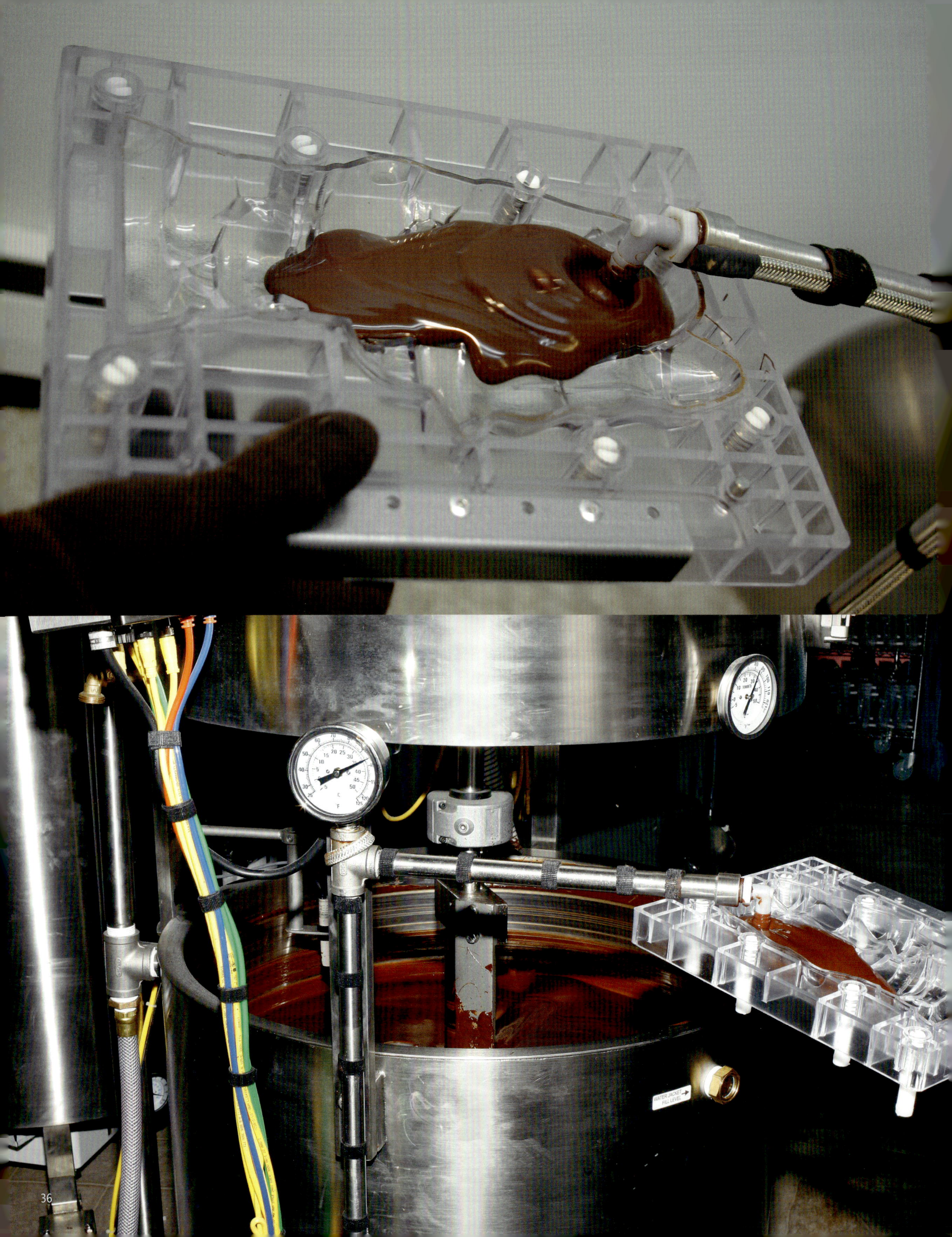
WATER JACKET
FILL LEVEL

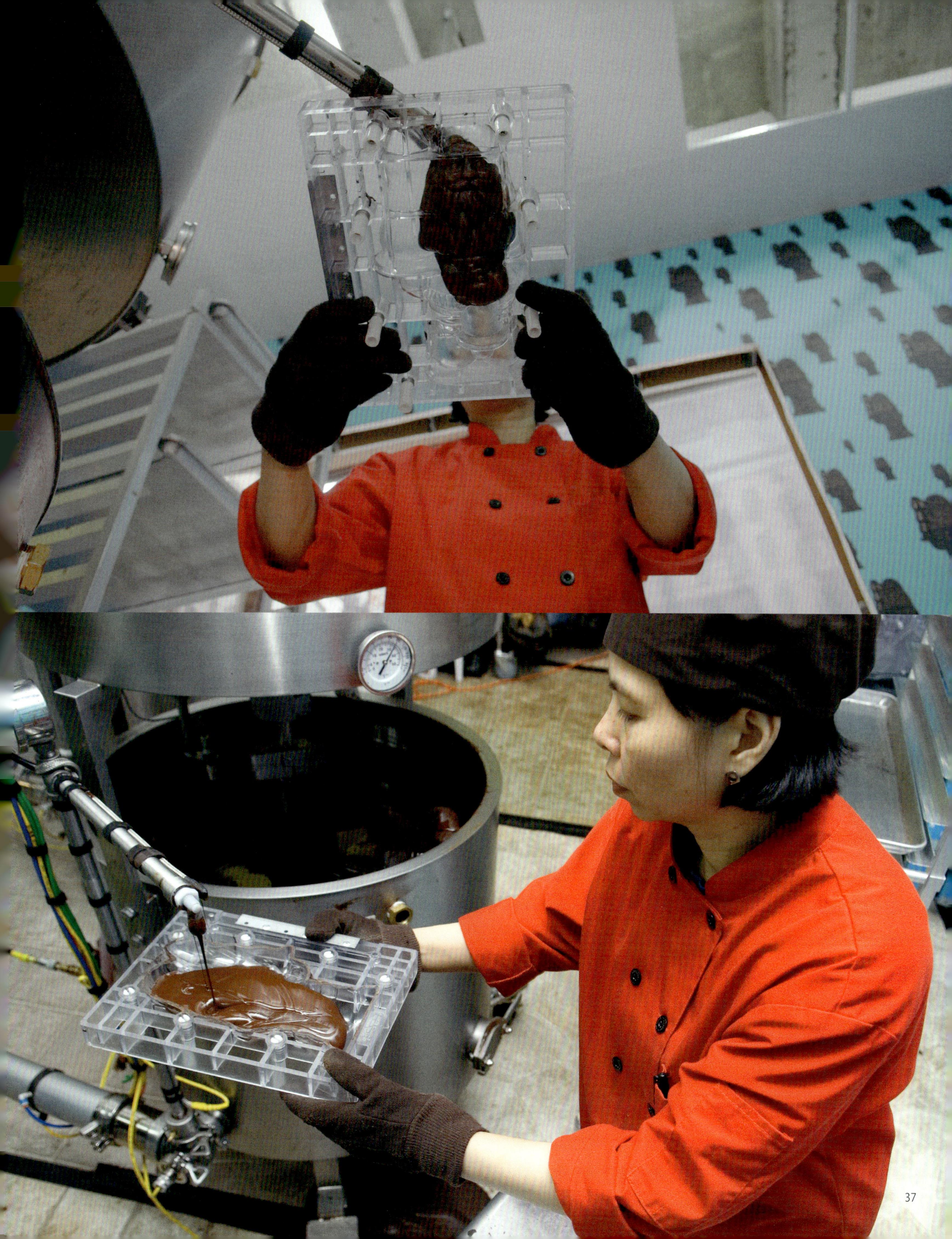

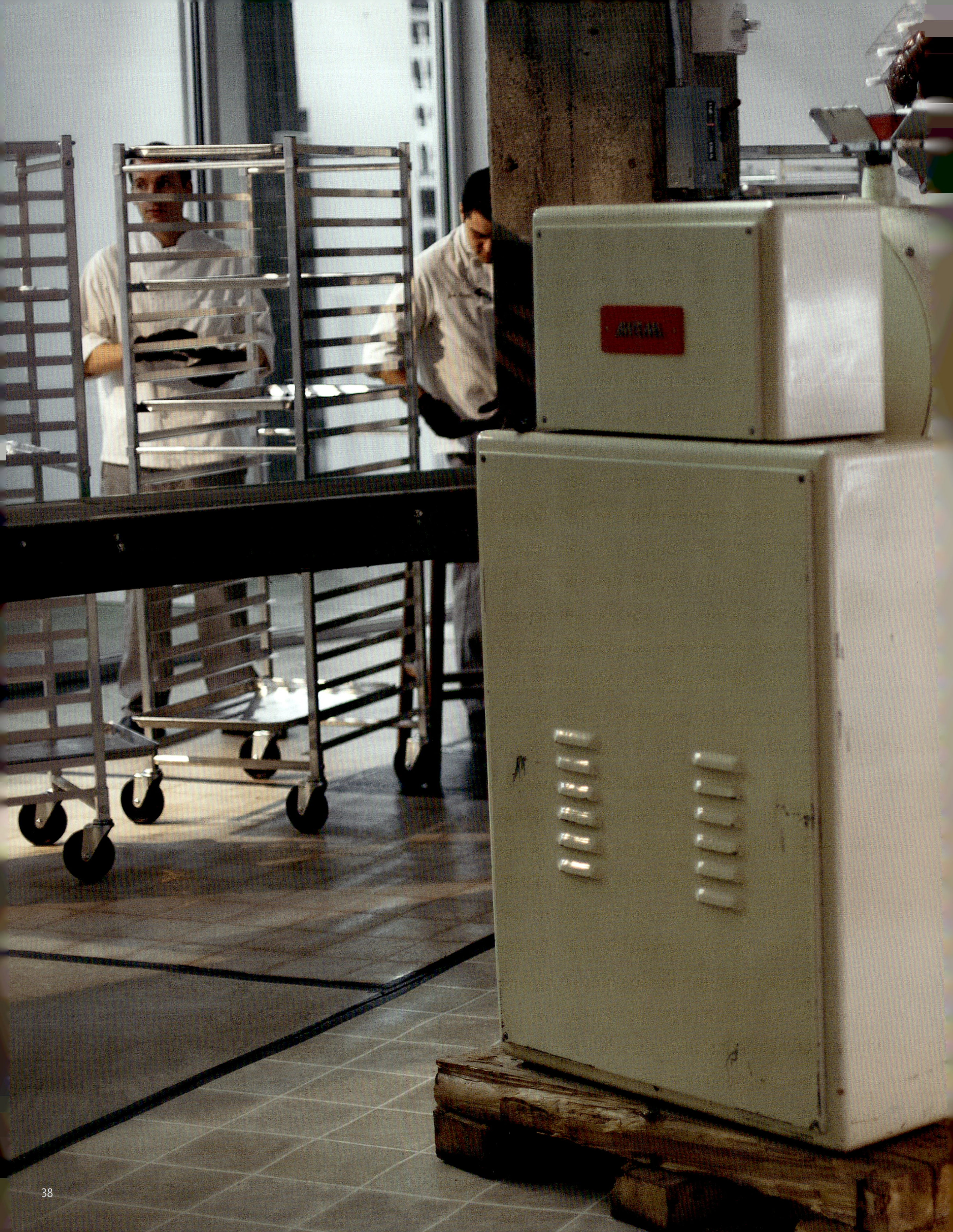

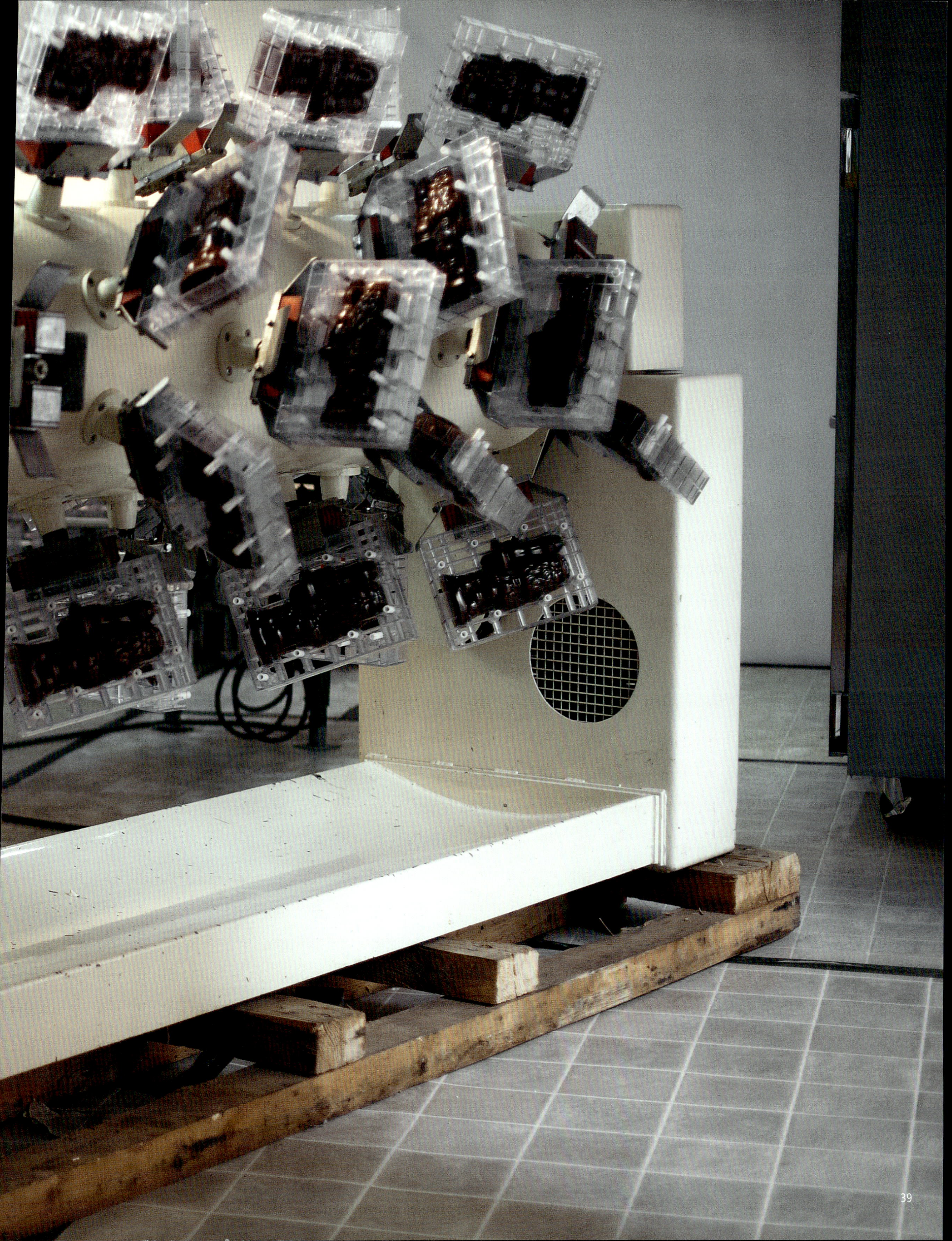

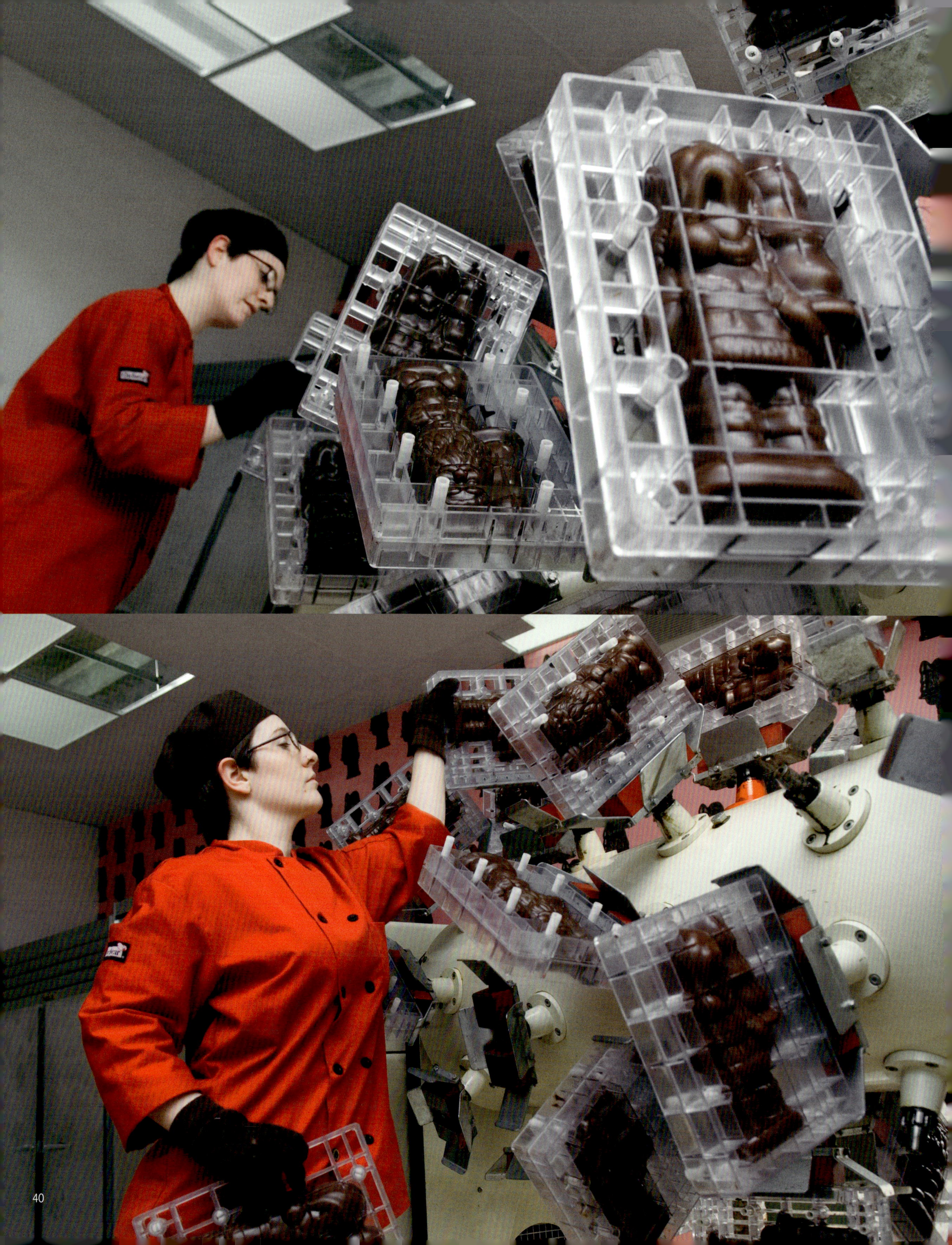

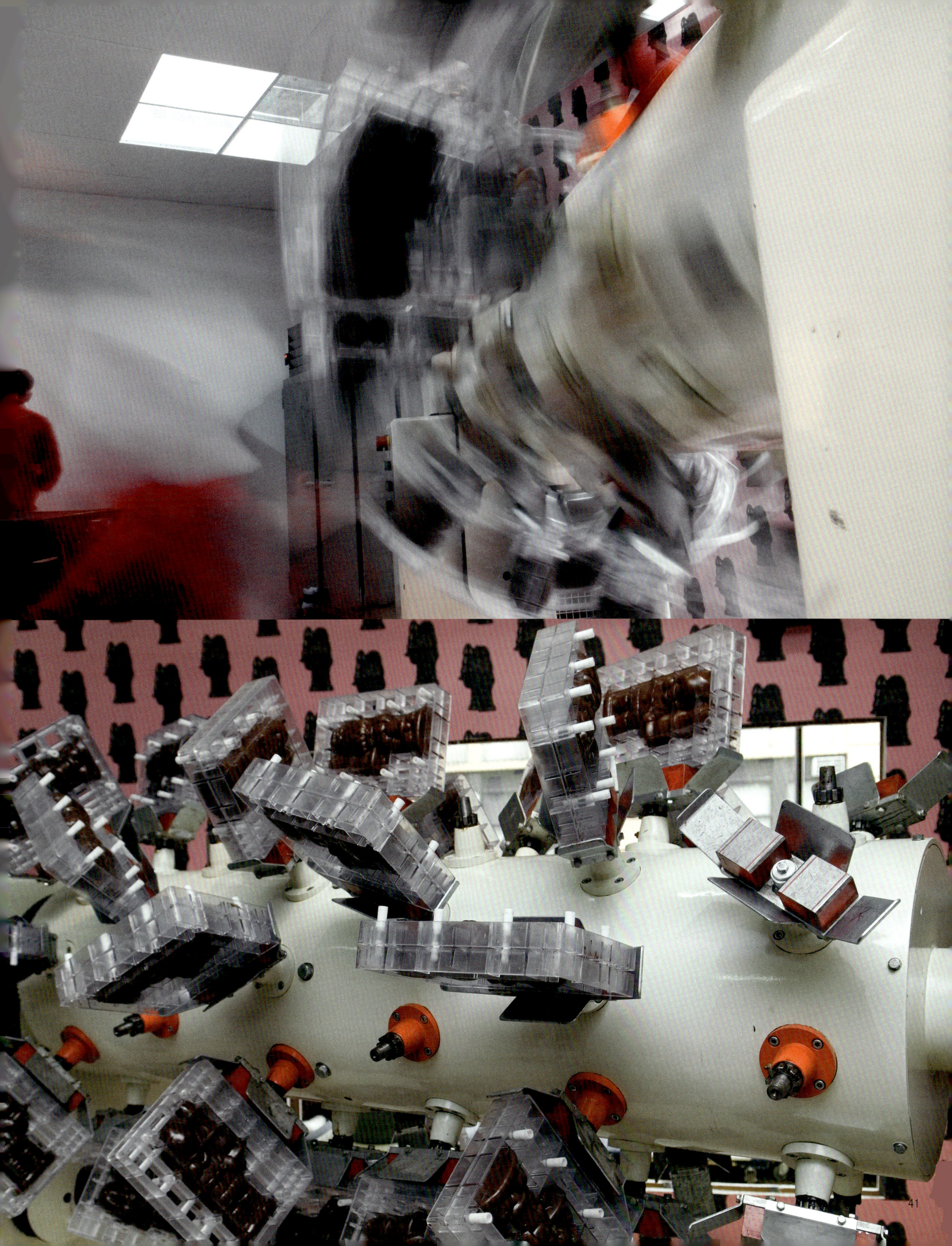

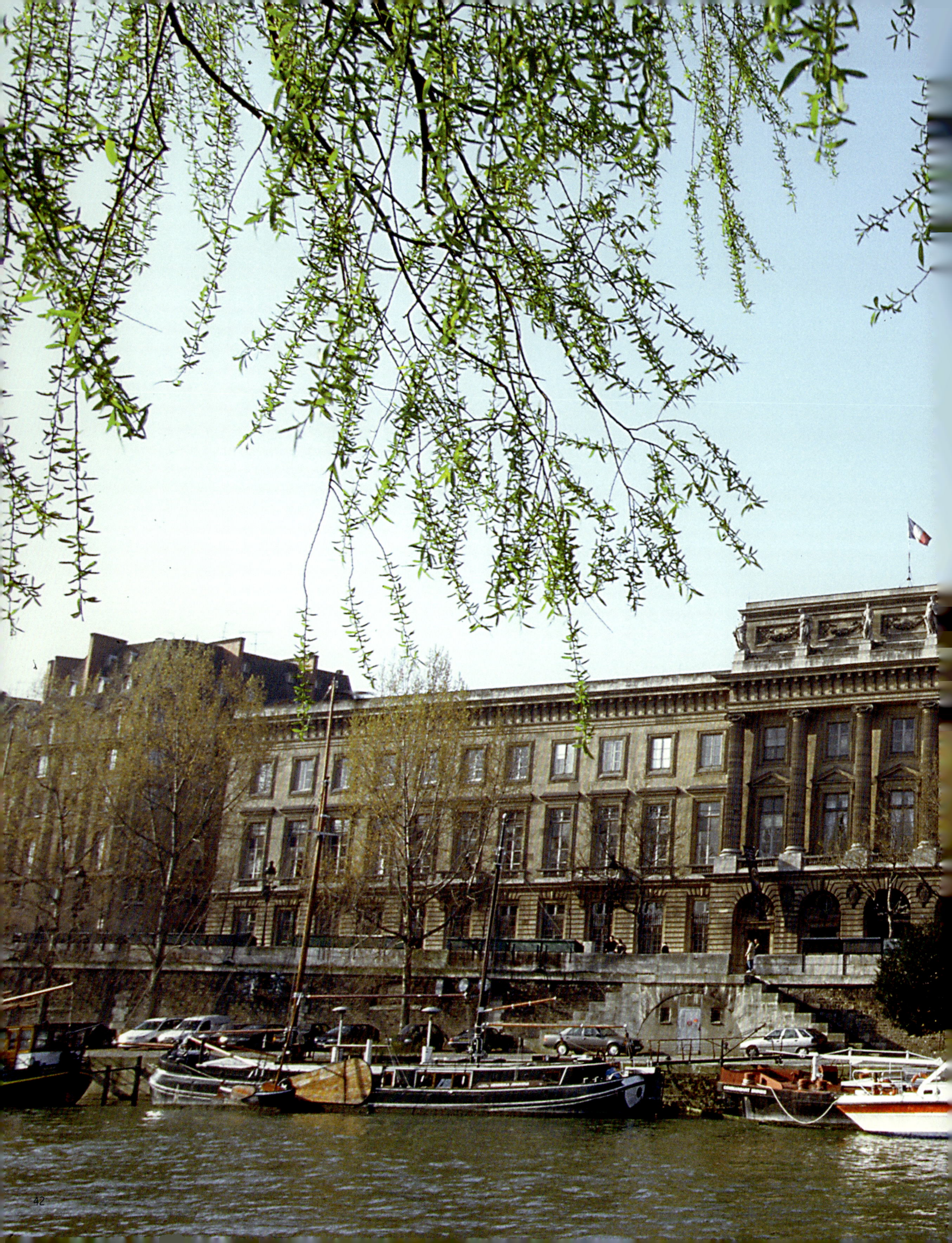

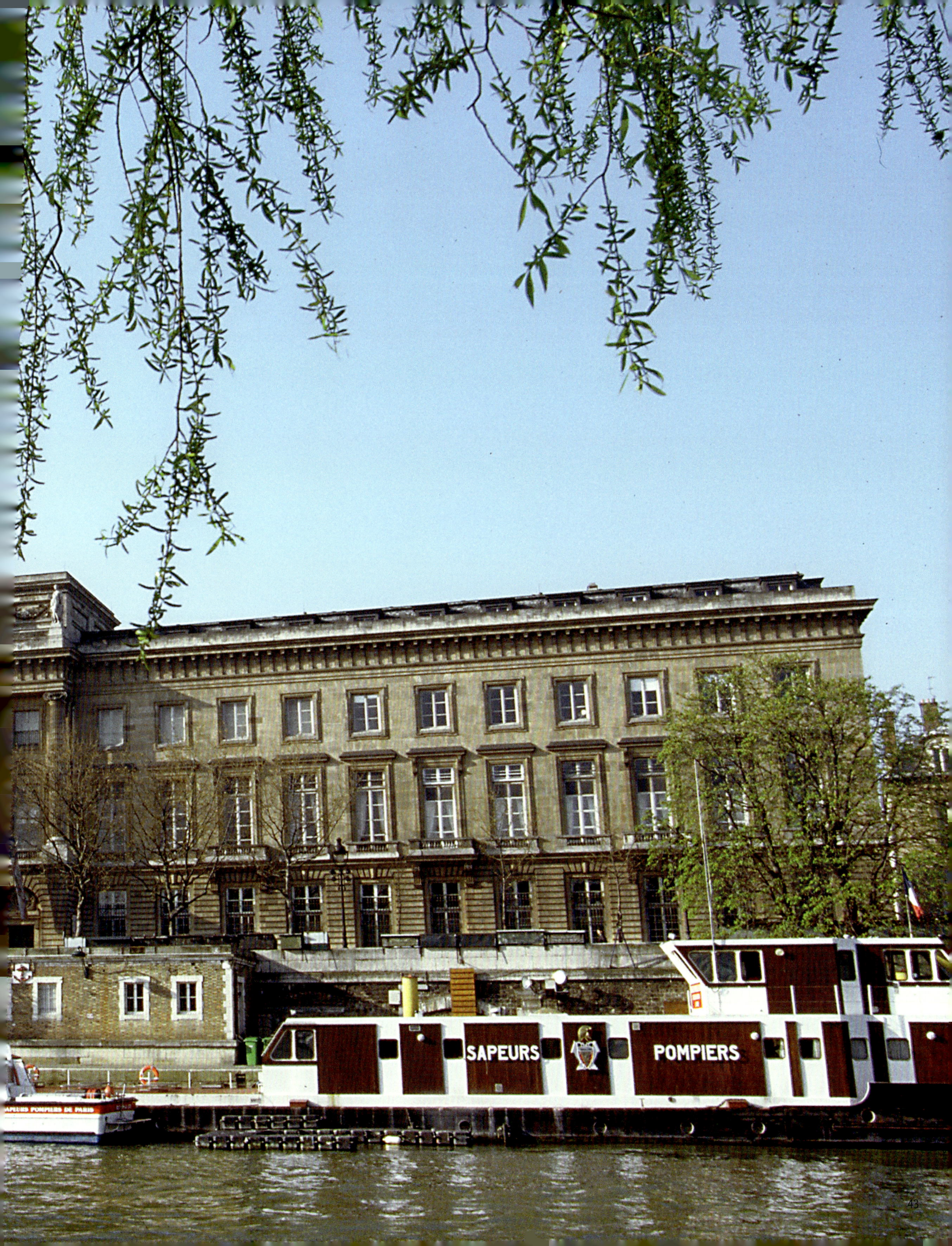
SAPEURS
POMPIERS

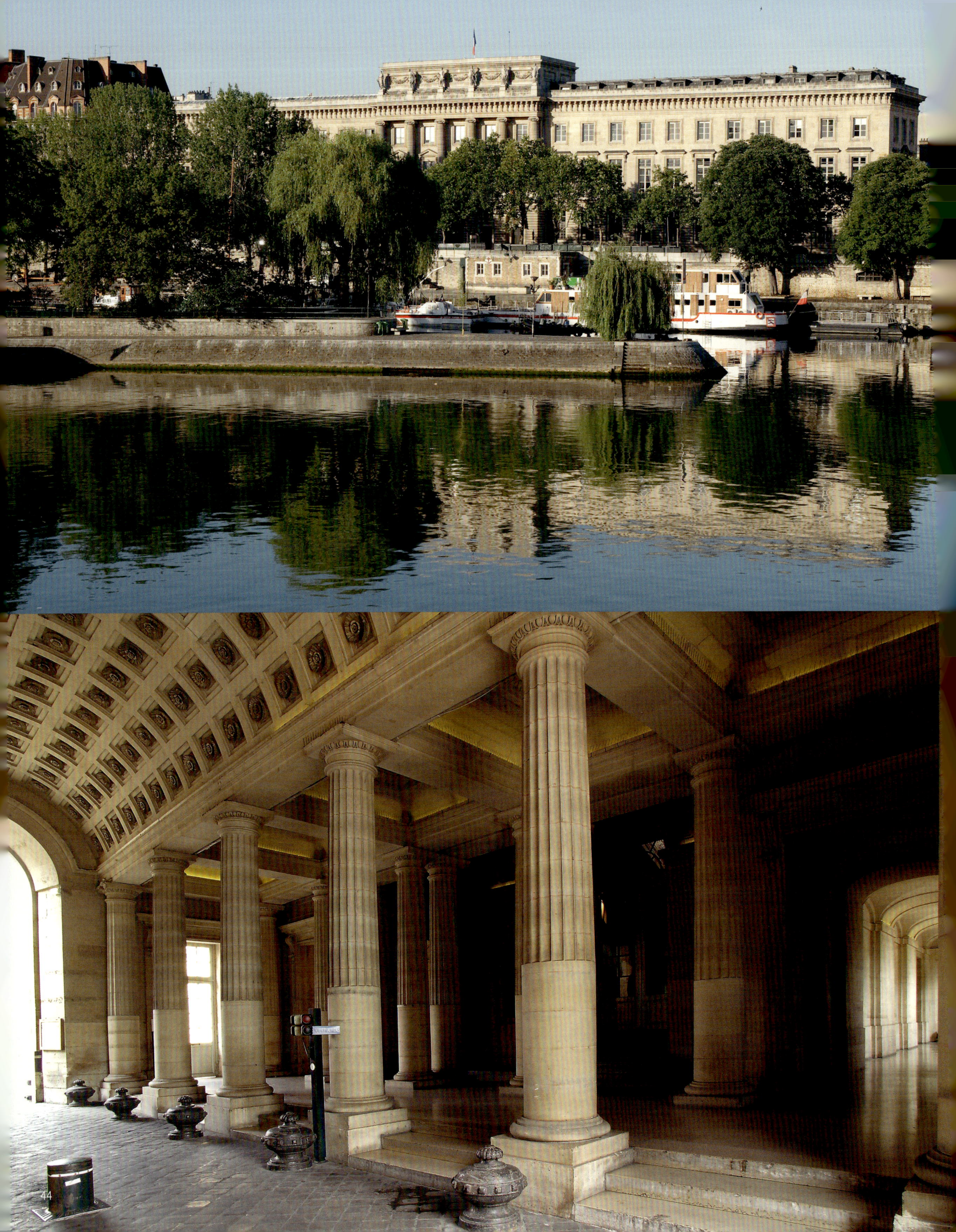

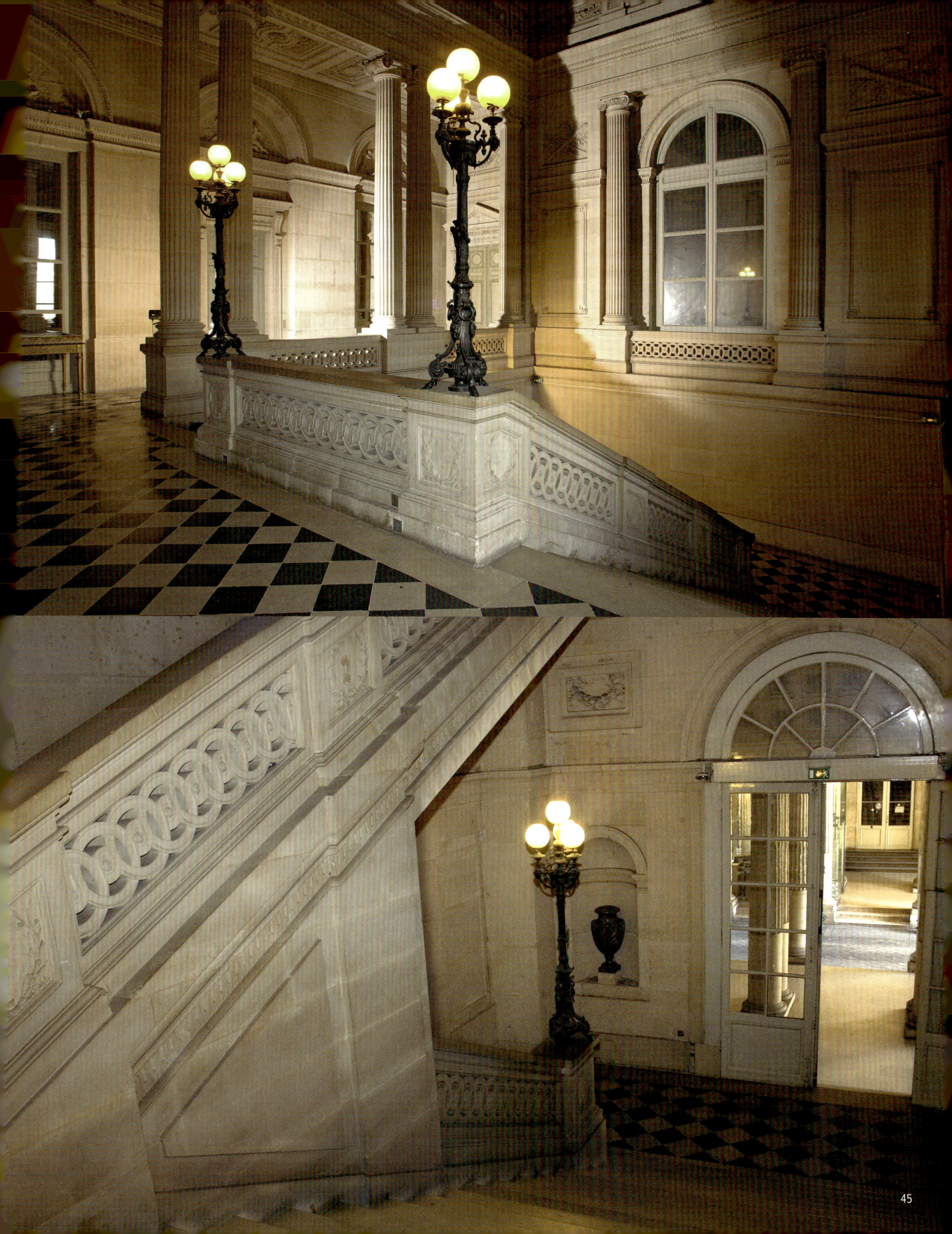

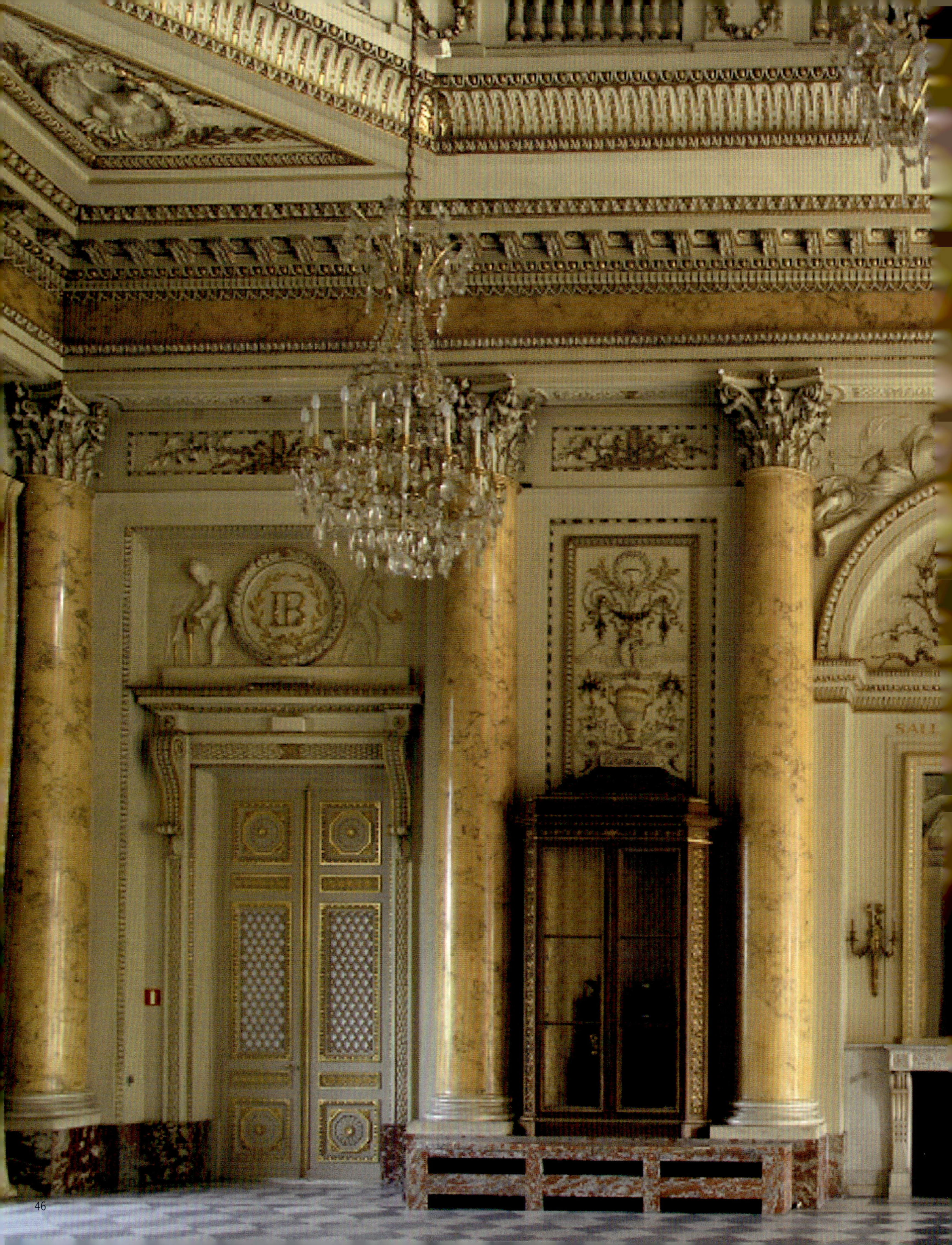

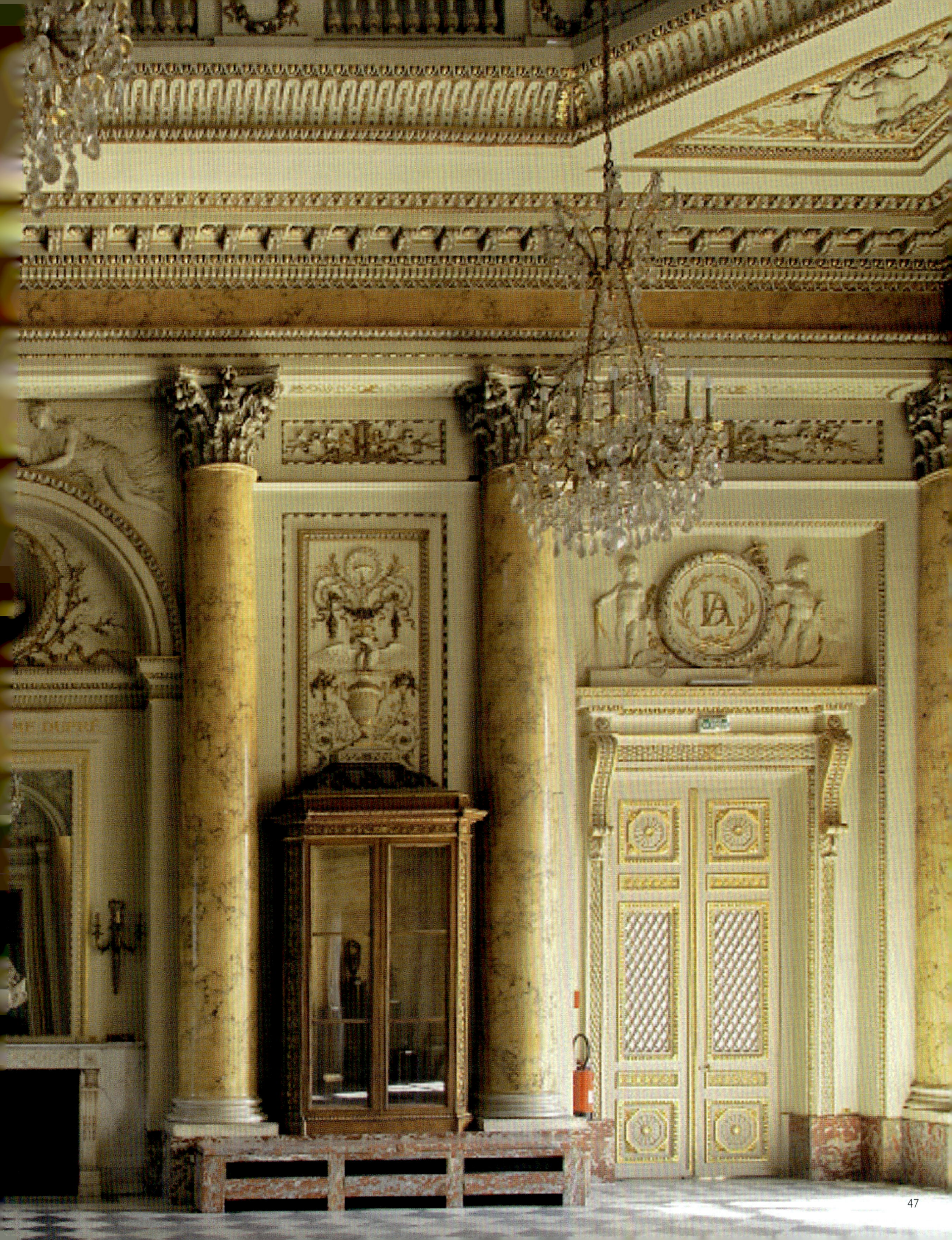

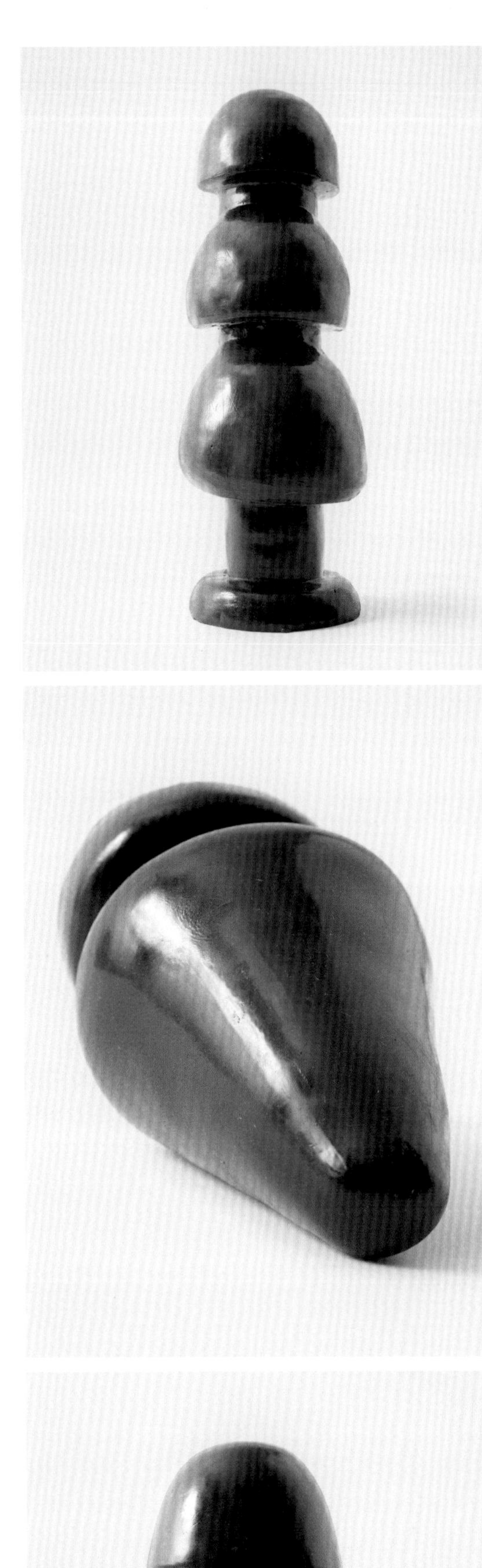

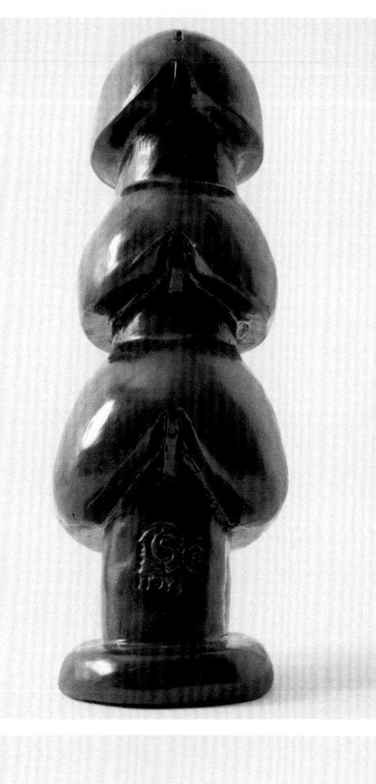

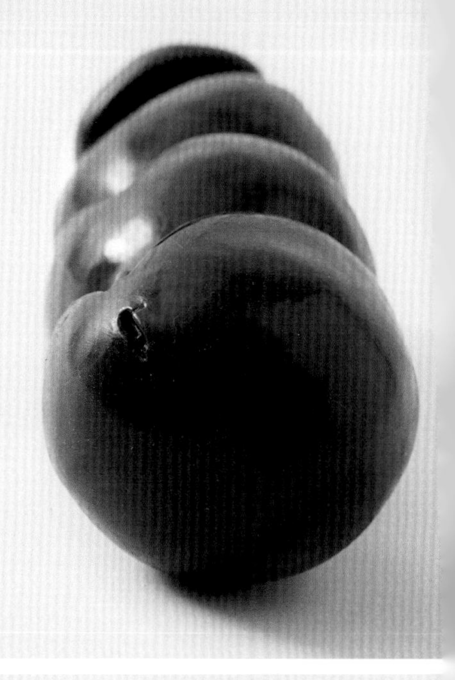

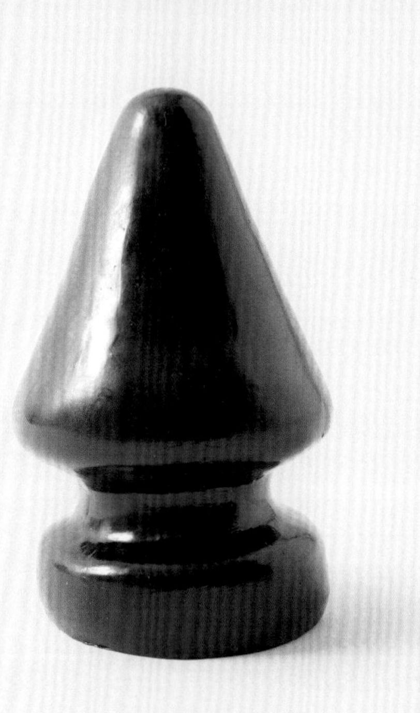

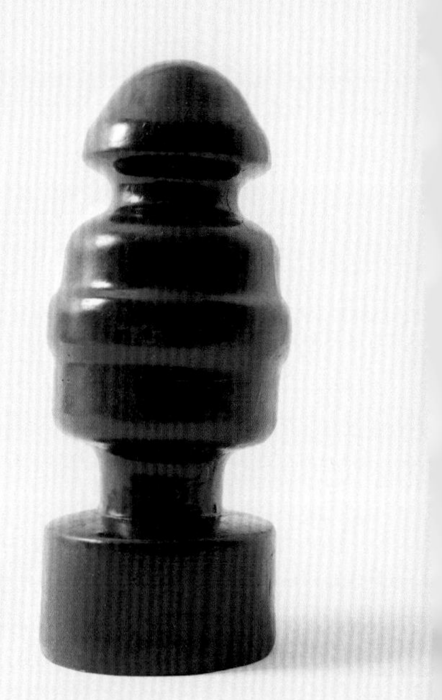

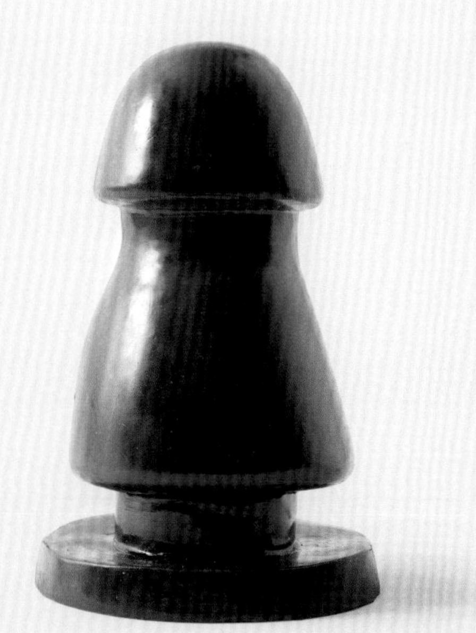

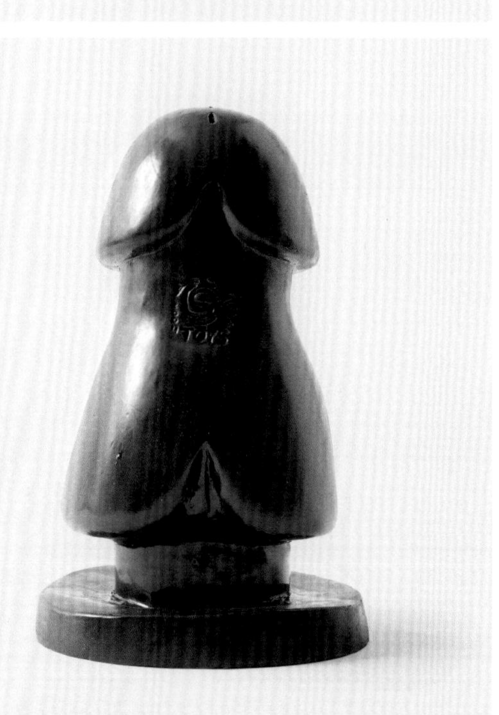

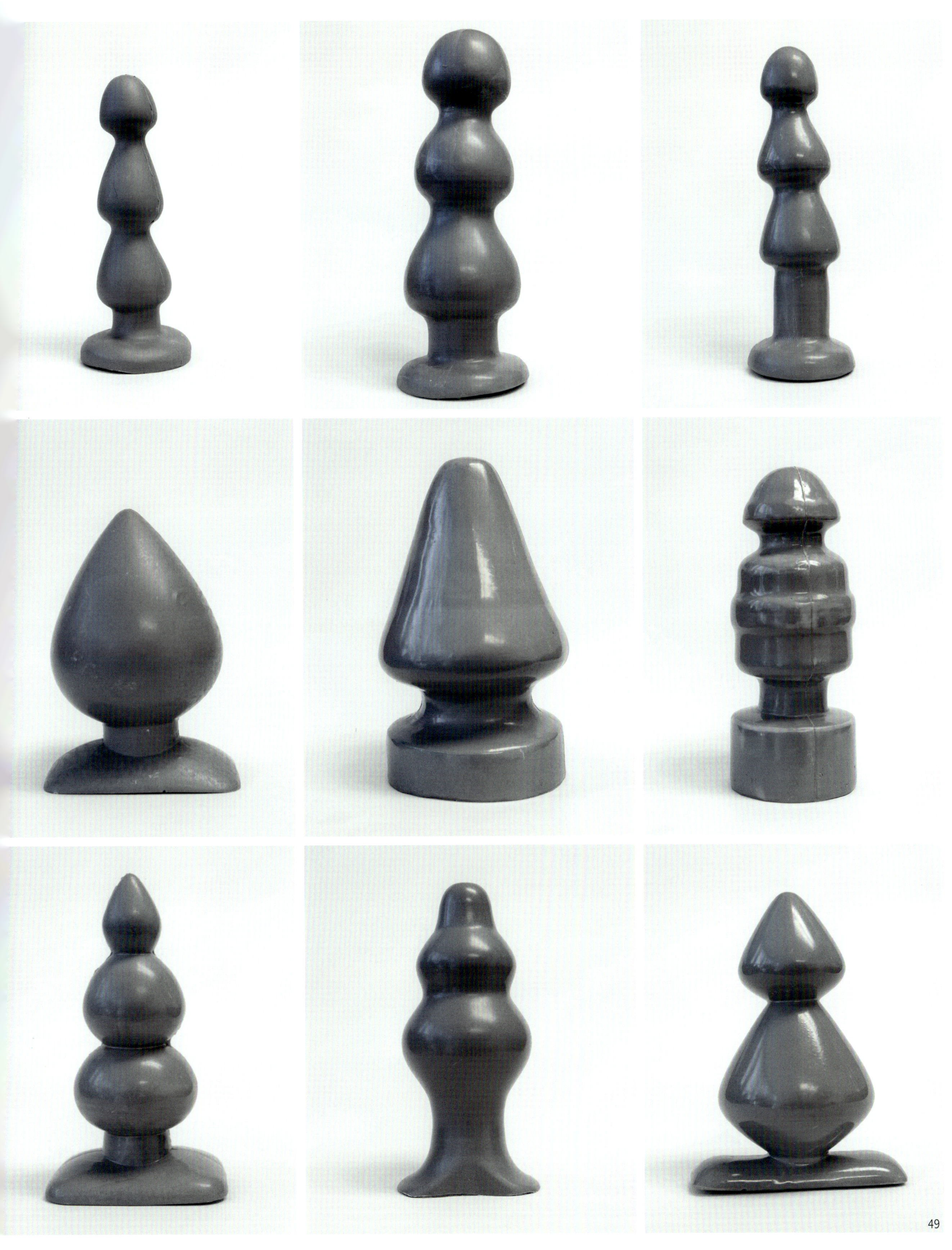

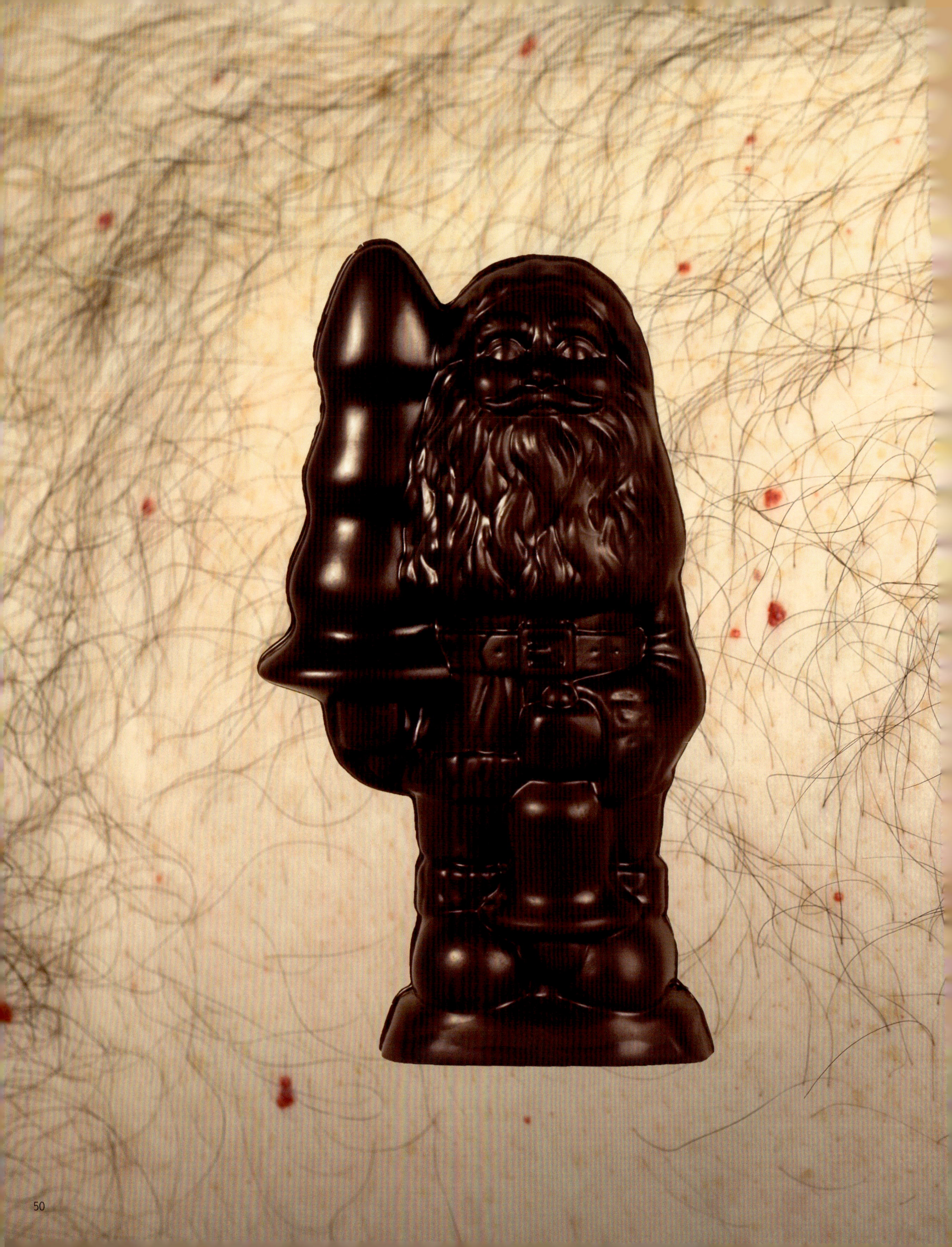

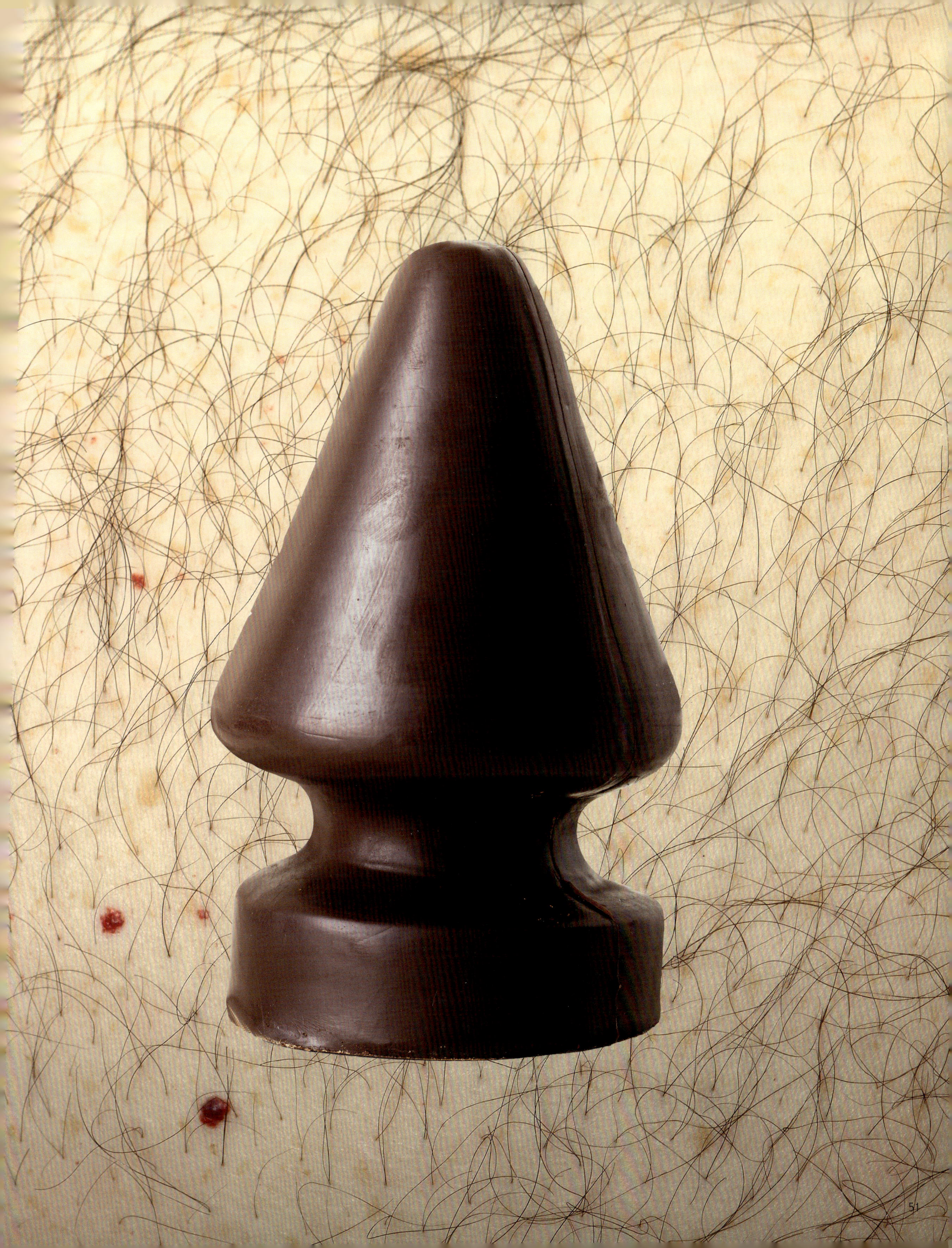

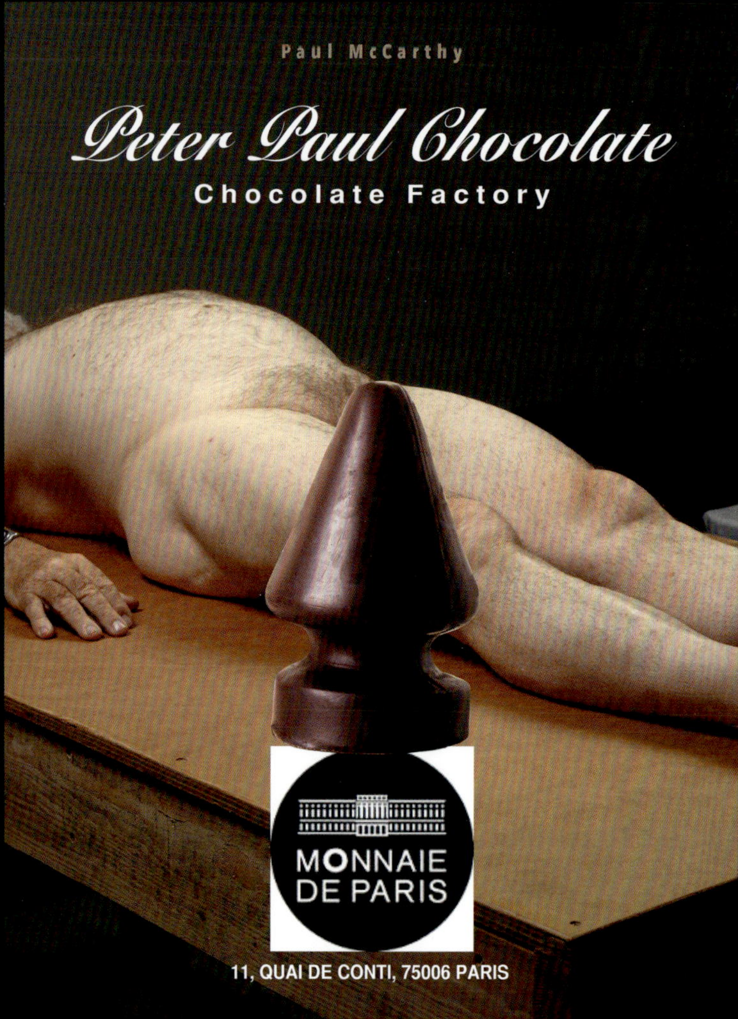
Paul McCarthy
Peter Paul Chocolate
Chocolate Factory
MONNAIE
DE PARIS
11, QUAI DE CONTI, 75006 PARIS

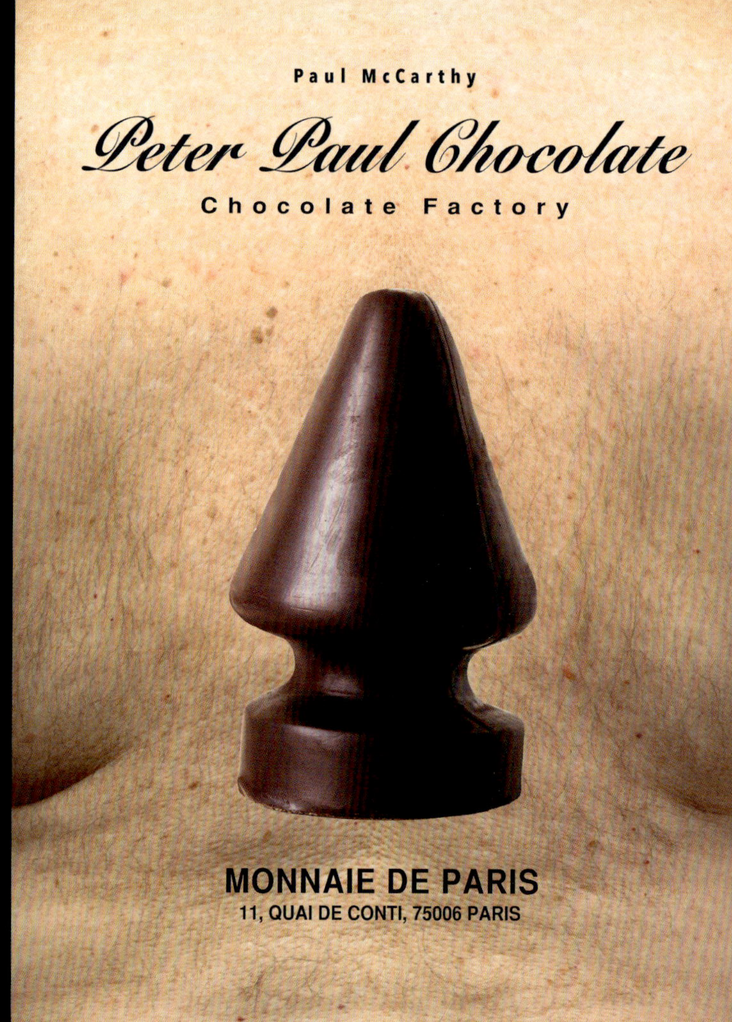
Paul McCarthy
Peter Paul Chocolate
Chocolate Factory
MONNAIE DE PARIS
11, QUAI DE CONTI, 75006 PARIS

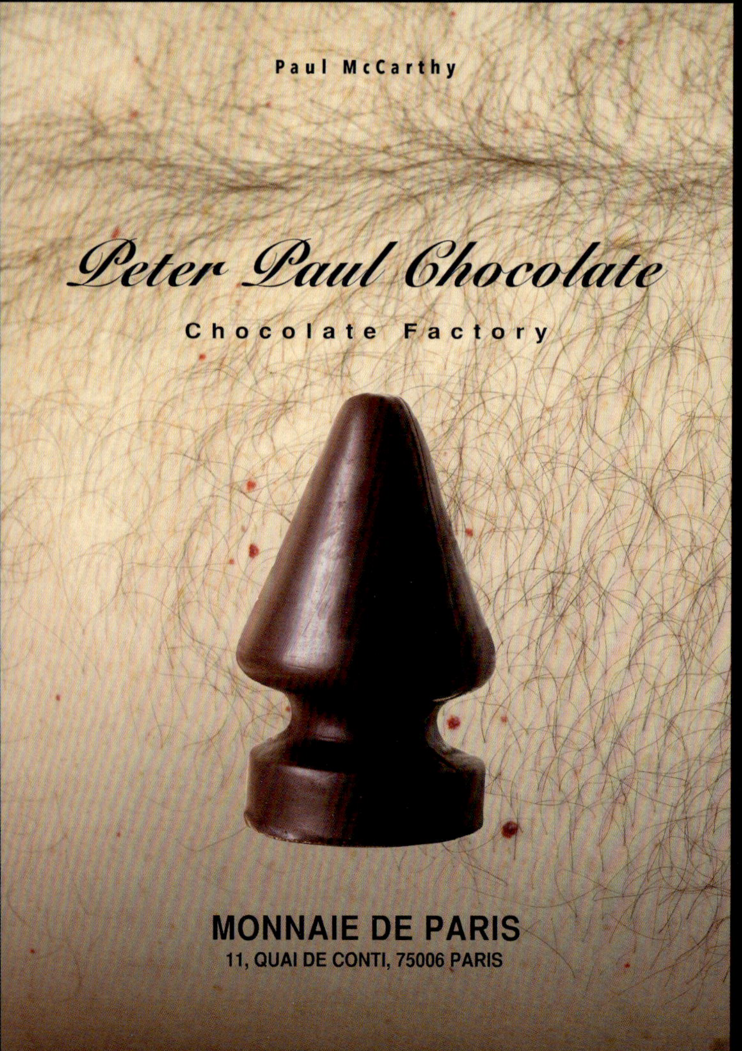
Paul McCarthy
Peter Paul Chocolate
Chocolate Factory
MONNAIE DE PARIS
11, QUAI DE CONTI, 75006 PARIS

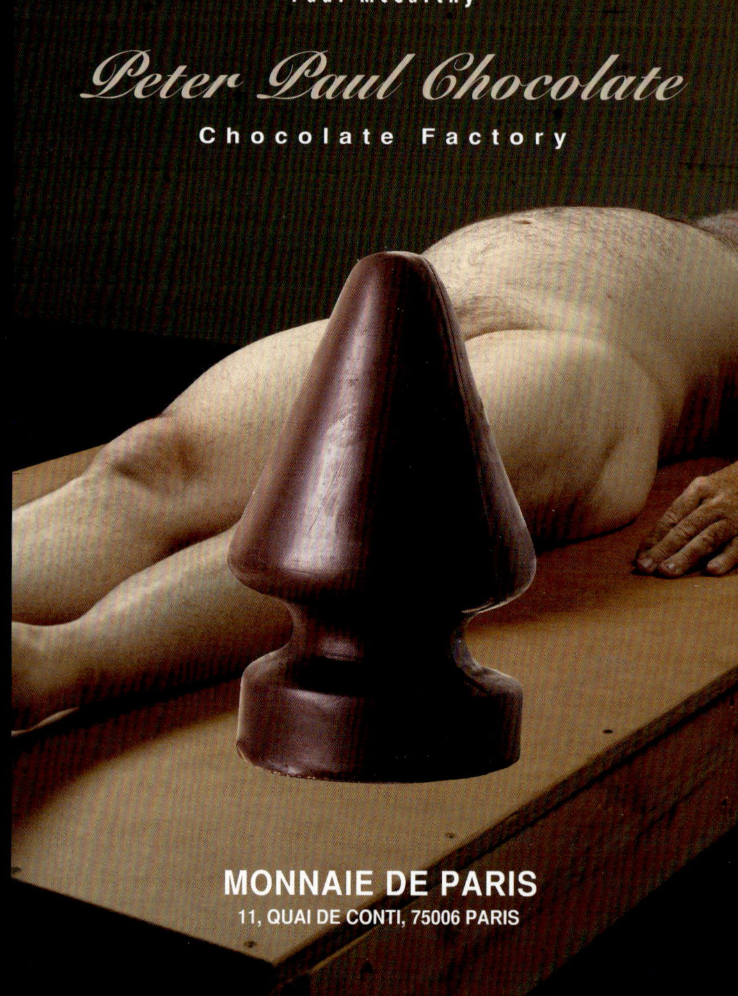
Paul McCarthy
Peter Paul Chocolate
Chocolate Factory
MONNAIE DE PARIS
11, QUAI DE CONTI, 75006 PARIS

Paul McCarthy

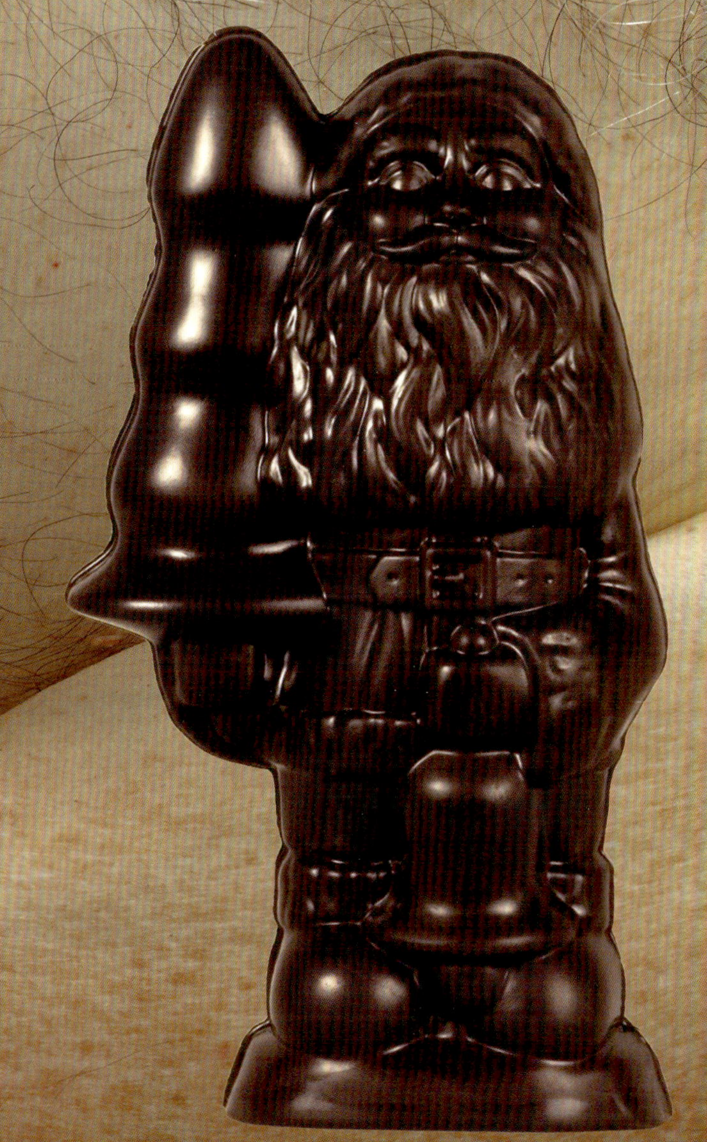

Peter Paul Chocolate

Chocolate Factory

MONNAIE DE PARIS

11, QUAI DE CONTI, 75006 PARIS

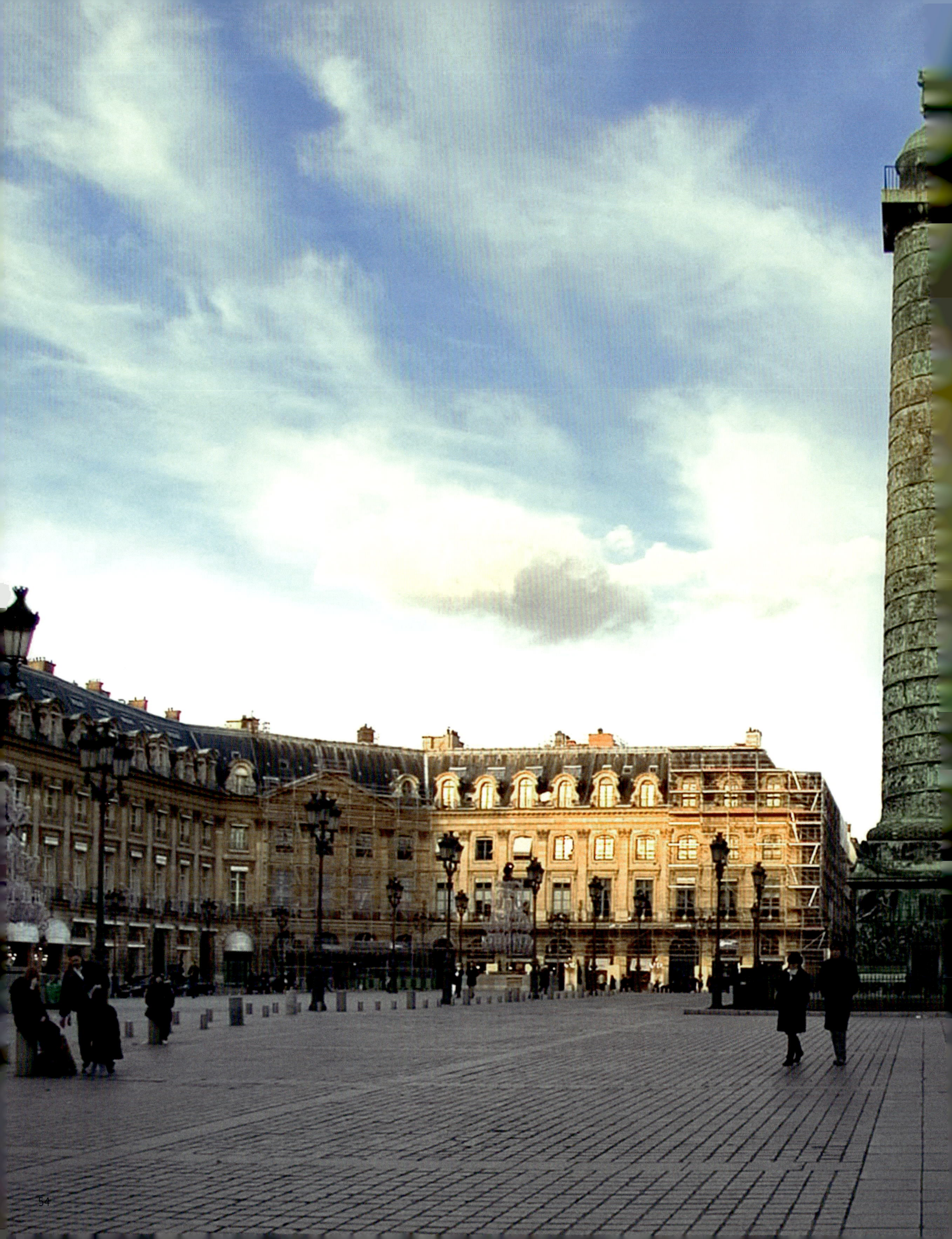

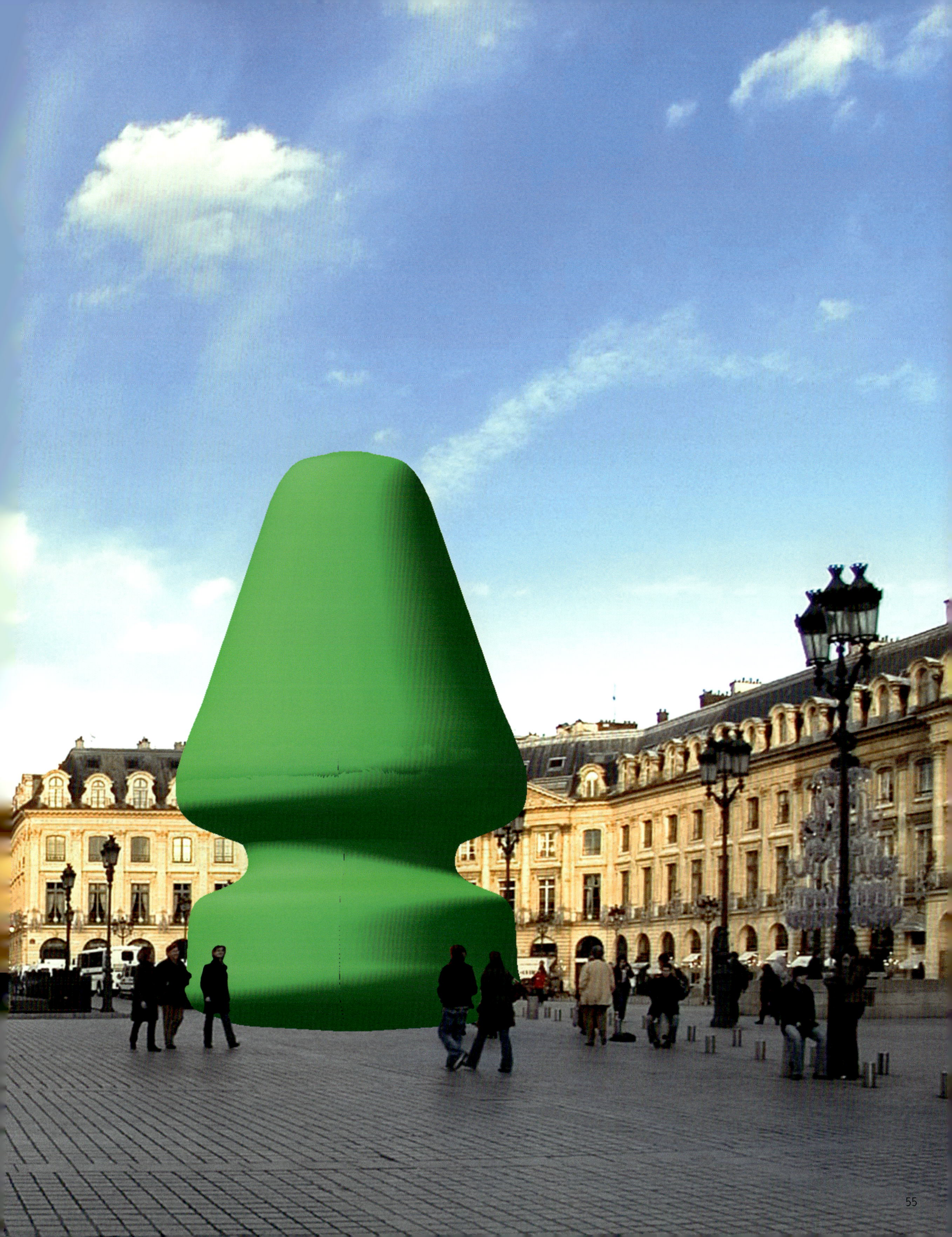

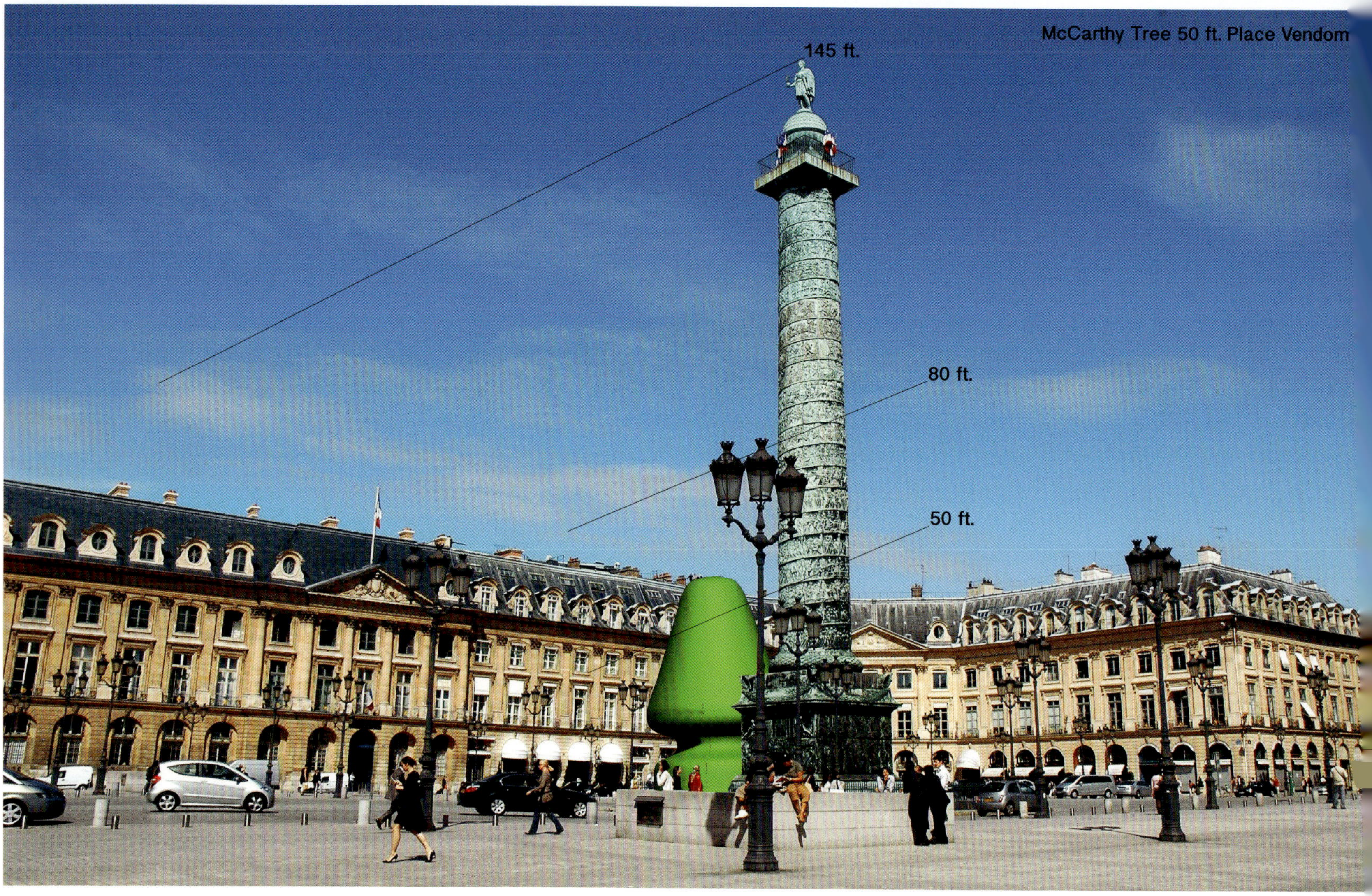

McCarthy Tree 50 ft. Place Vendom

145 ft.

80 ft.

50 ft.

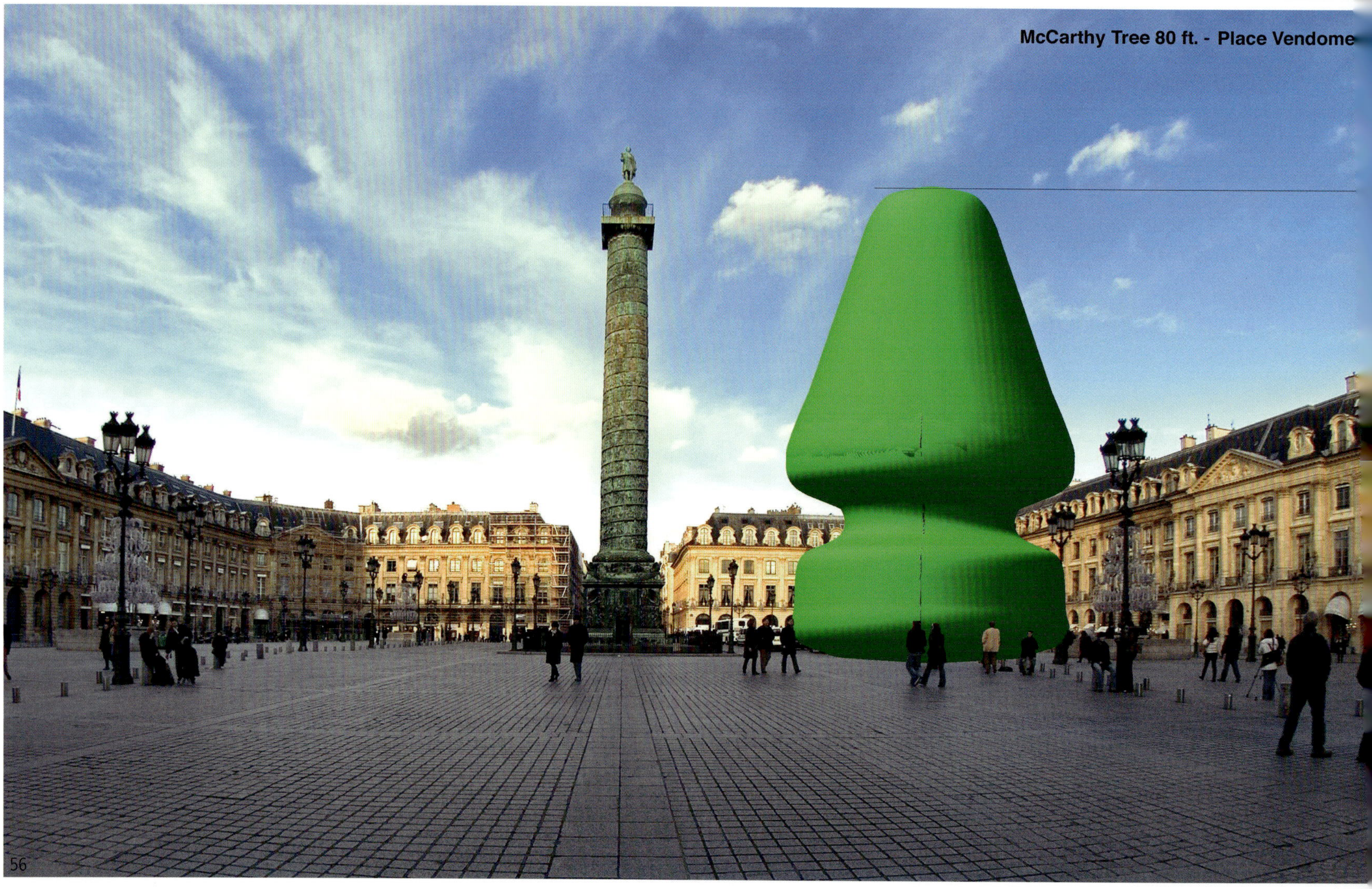

McCarthy Tree 80 ft. - Place Vendome

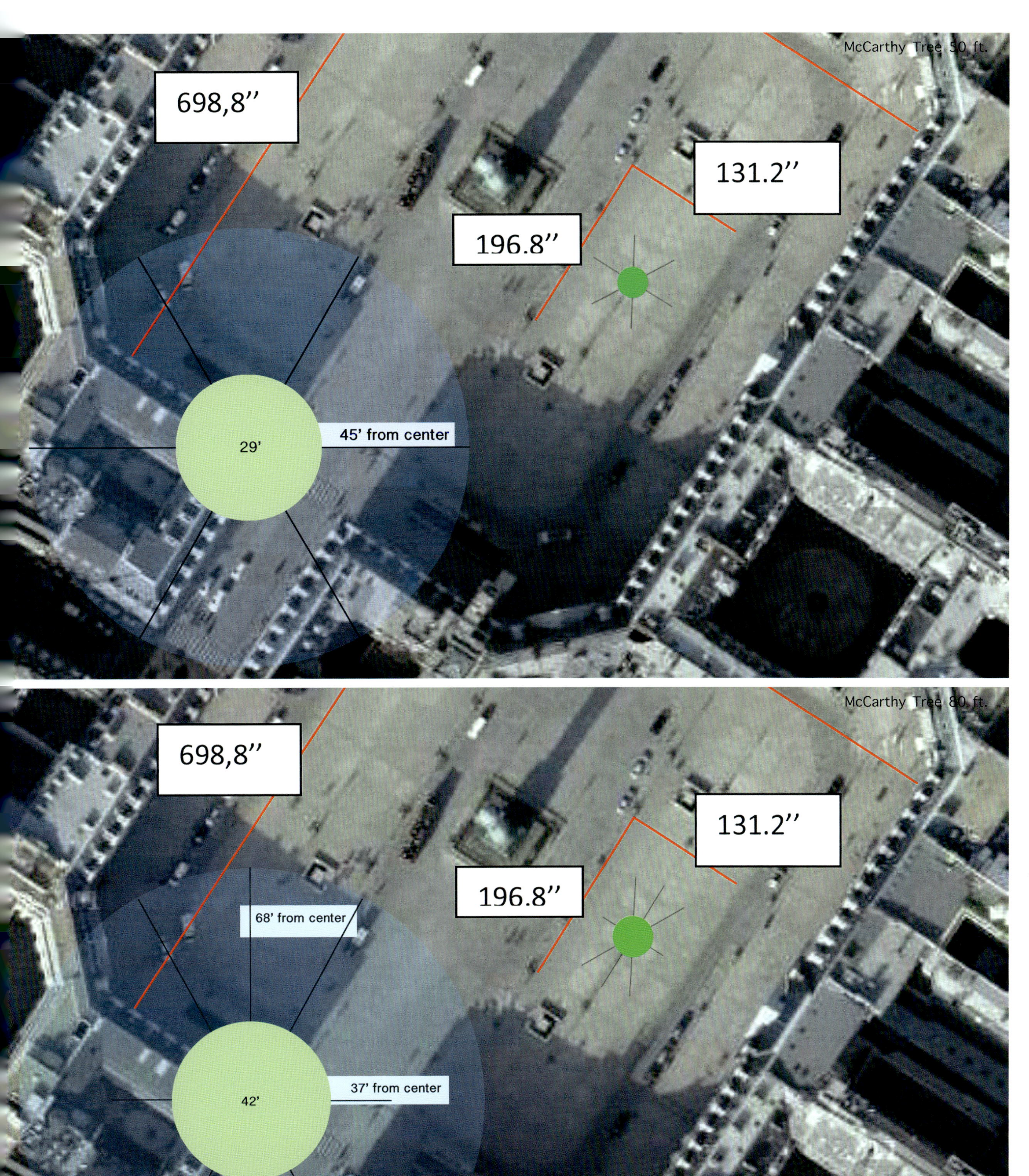
McCarthy Tree 50 ft.
698,8’’
131.2’’
196.8’’
45’ from center
29’
McCarthy Tree 80 ft.
698,8’’
131.2’’
196.8’’
68’ from center
37’ from center
42’

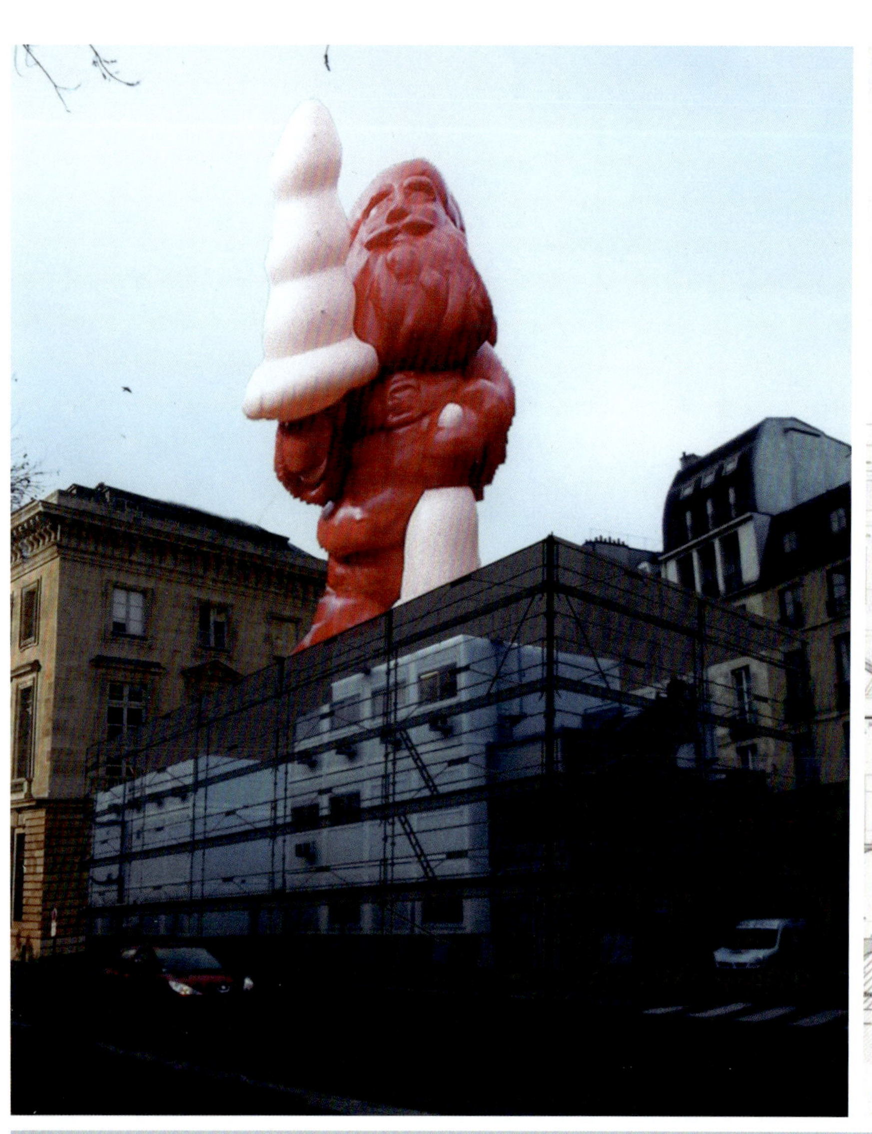

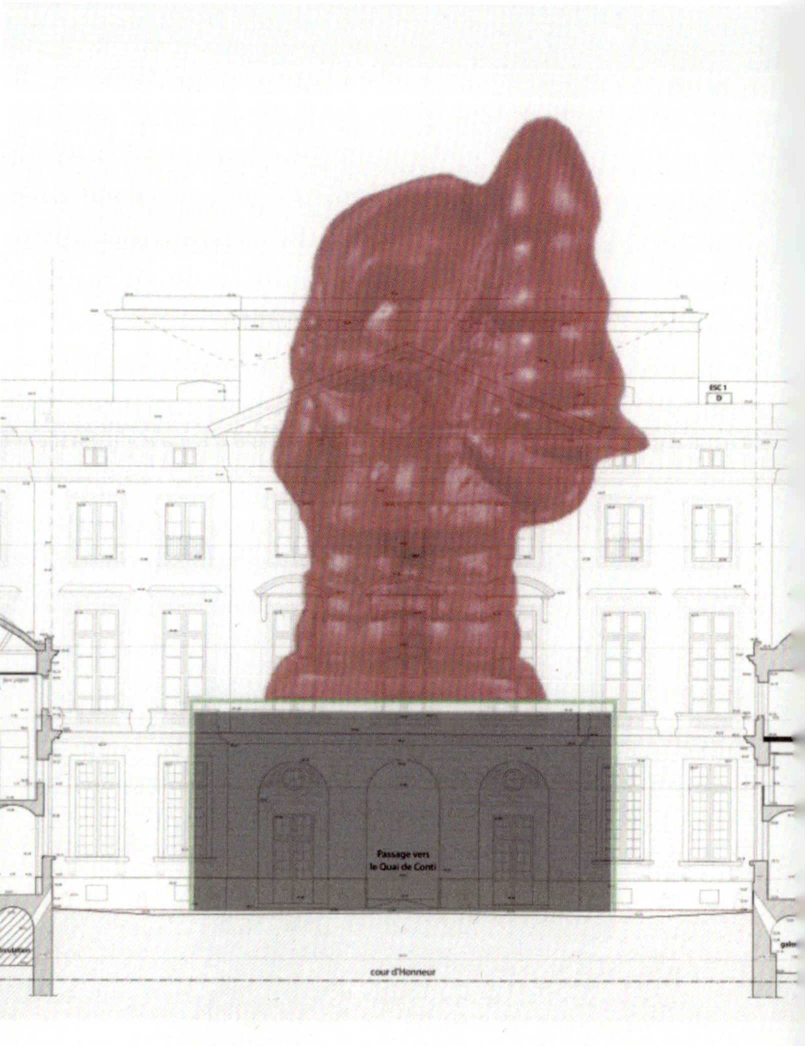
Passage vers
le Quai de Conti
cour d'Honneur

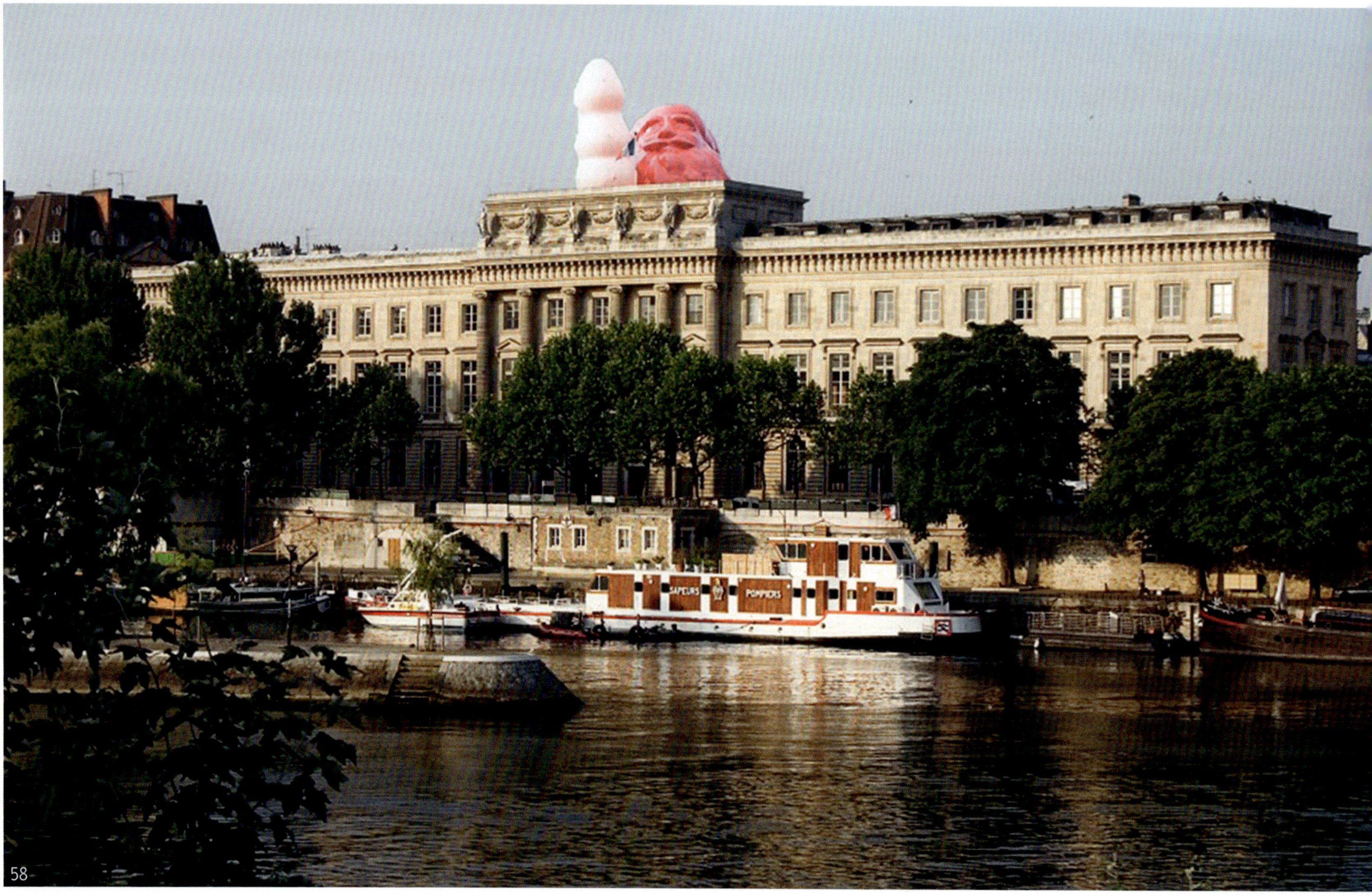

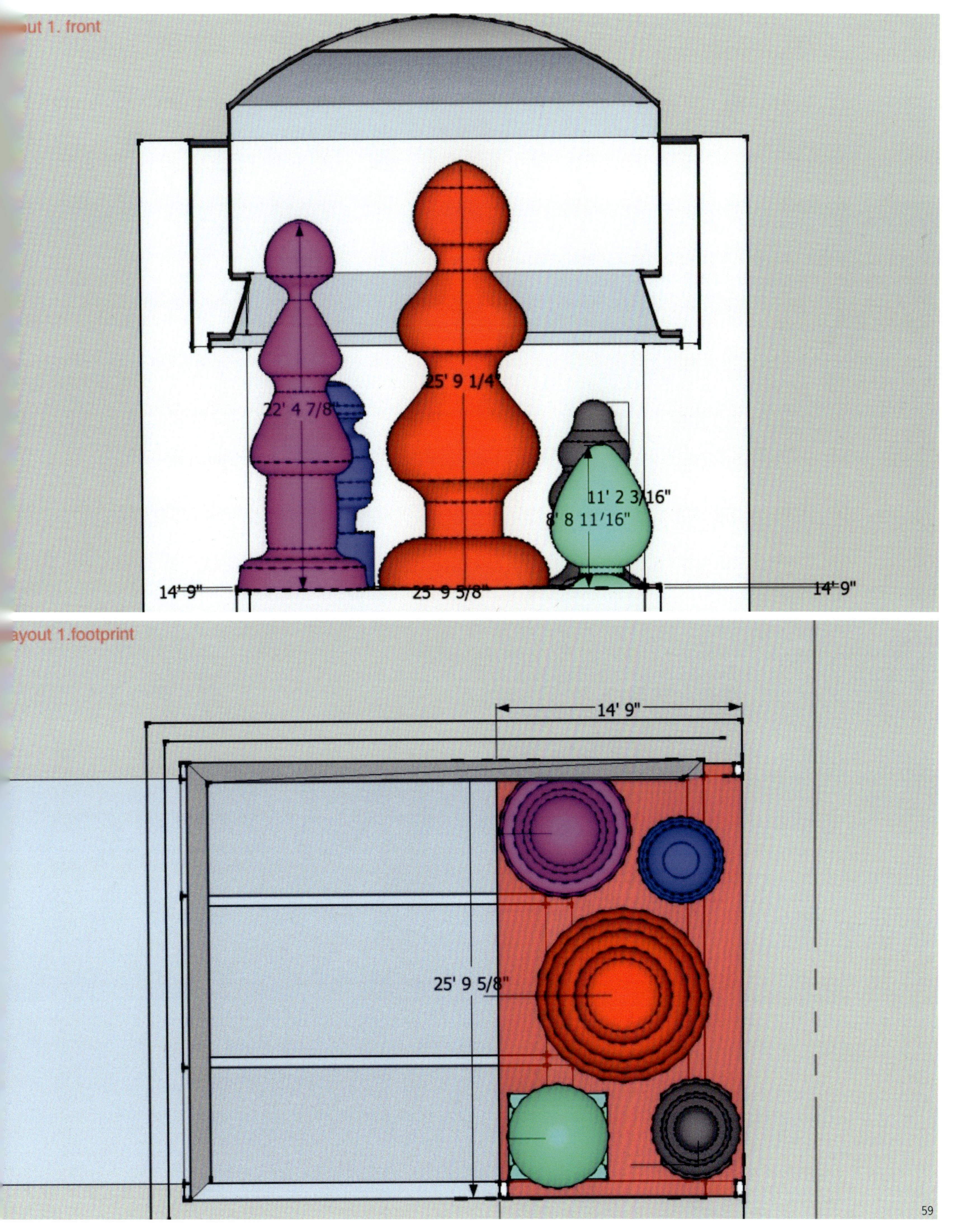

ut 1. front
22' 4 7/8"
25' 9 1/4"
11' 2 3/16"
8' 8 11/16"
14' 9"
25' 9 5/8"
14' 9"
ayout 1.footprint
14' 9"
25' 9 5/8"

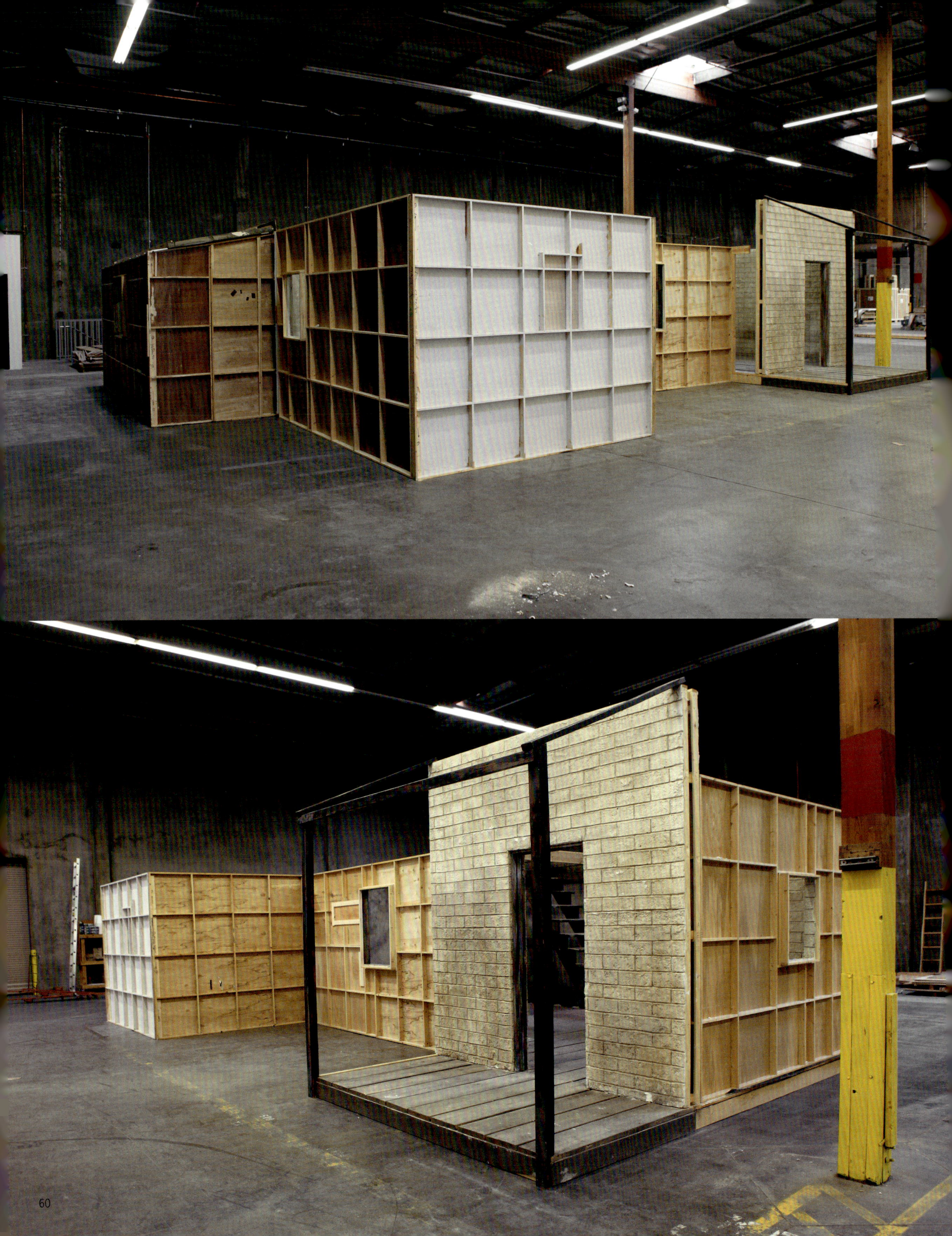

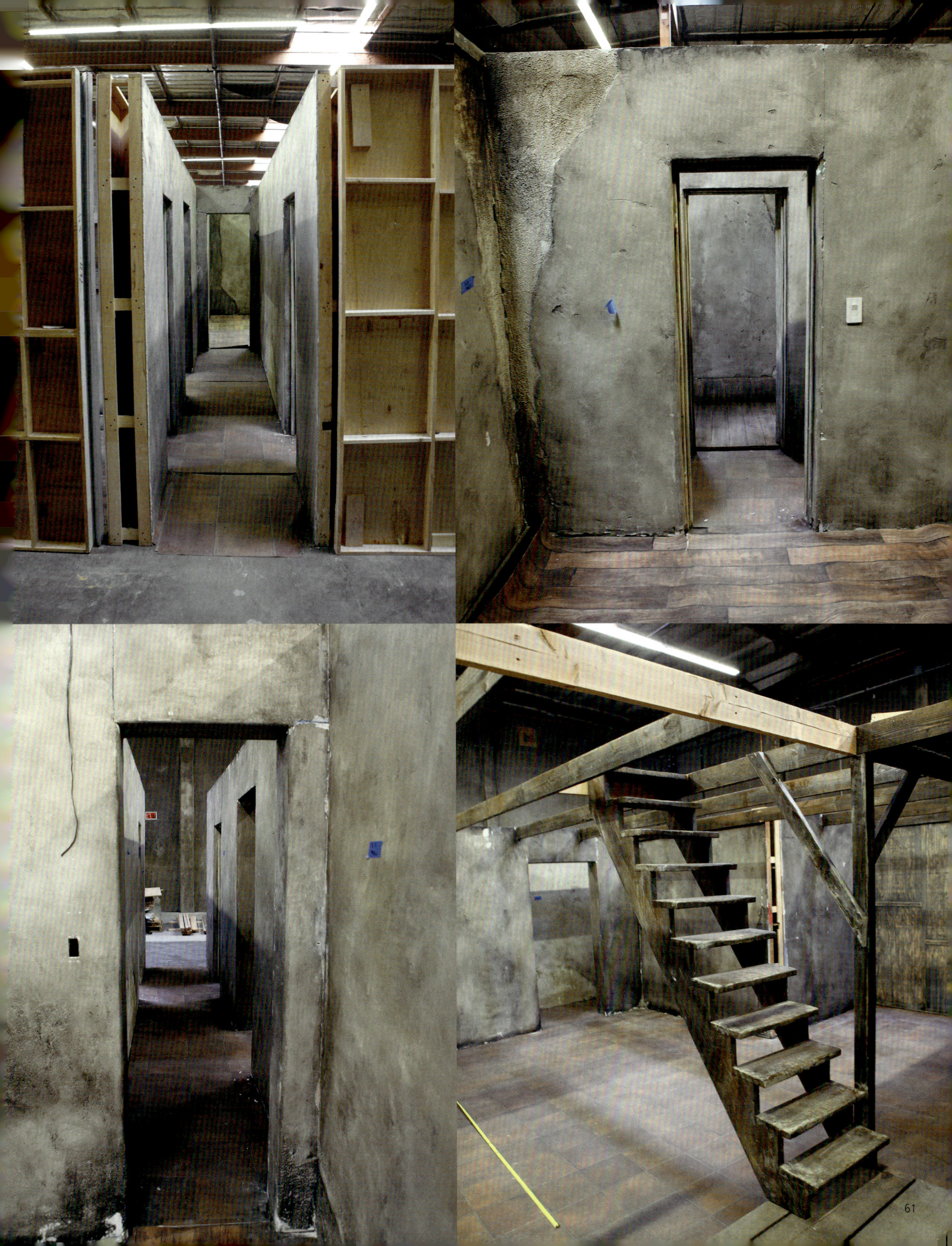

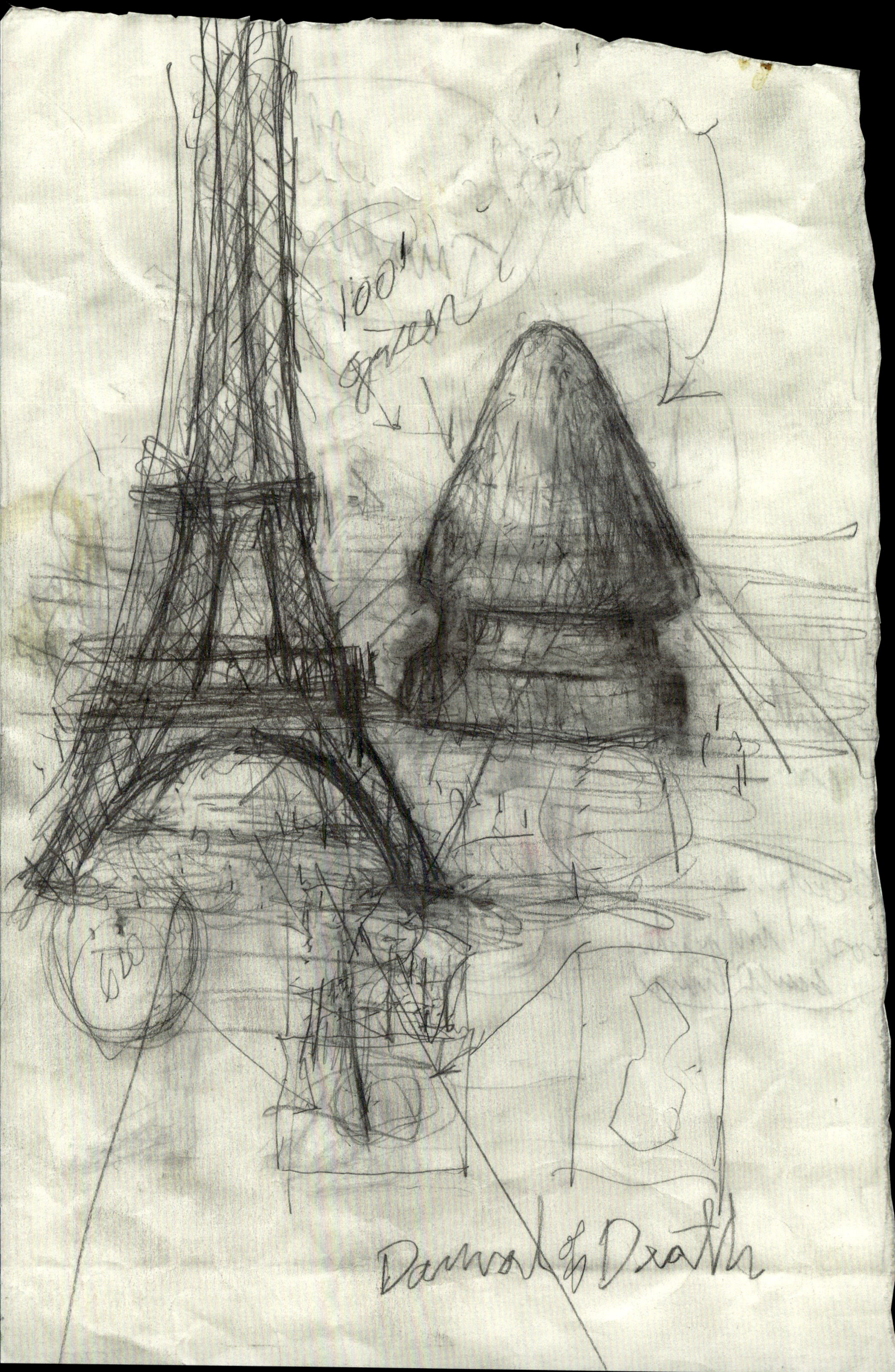
100'
green

chocolate factory
Party Life
chocolate sculpture
chocolate as shit
shit as chocolate

chocolate
Plug

chocolate

chocolate
Plug

chocolate
Red Carpet
Mall Mess

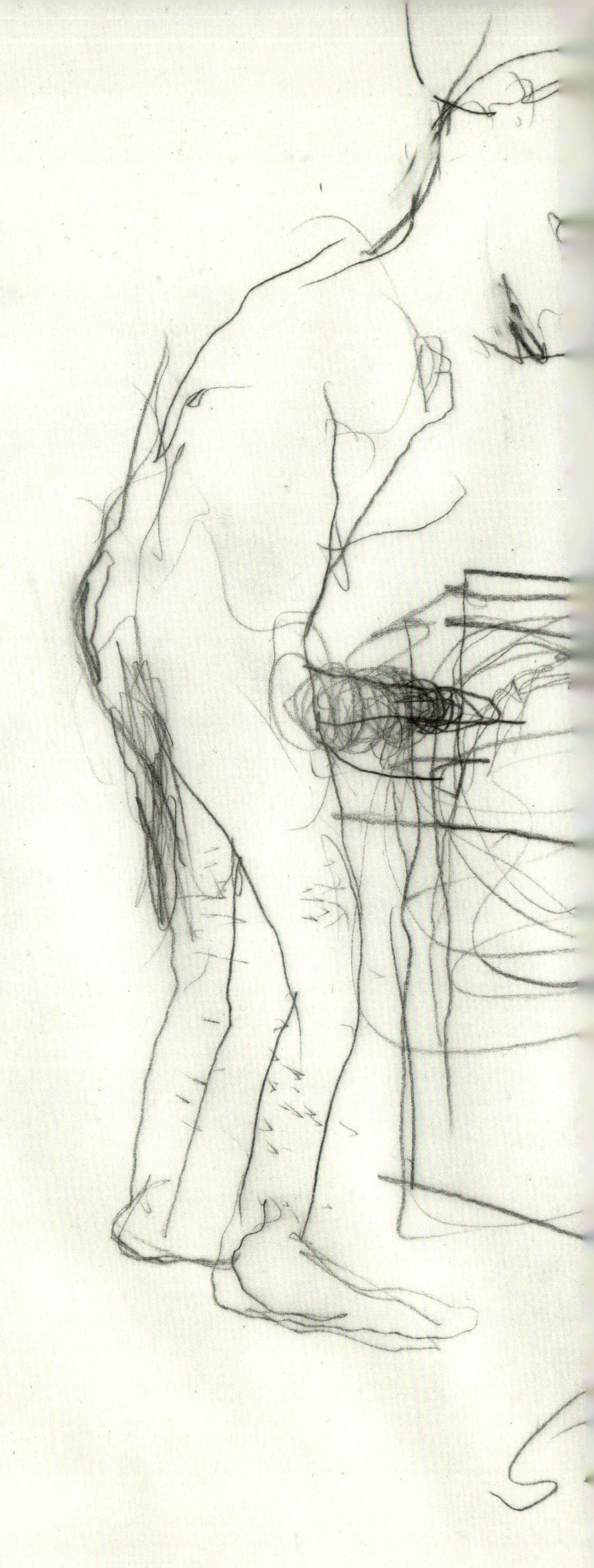

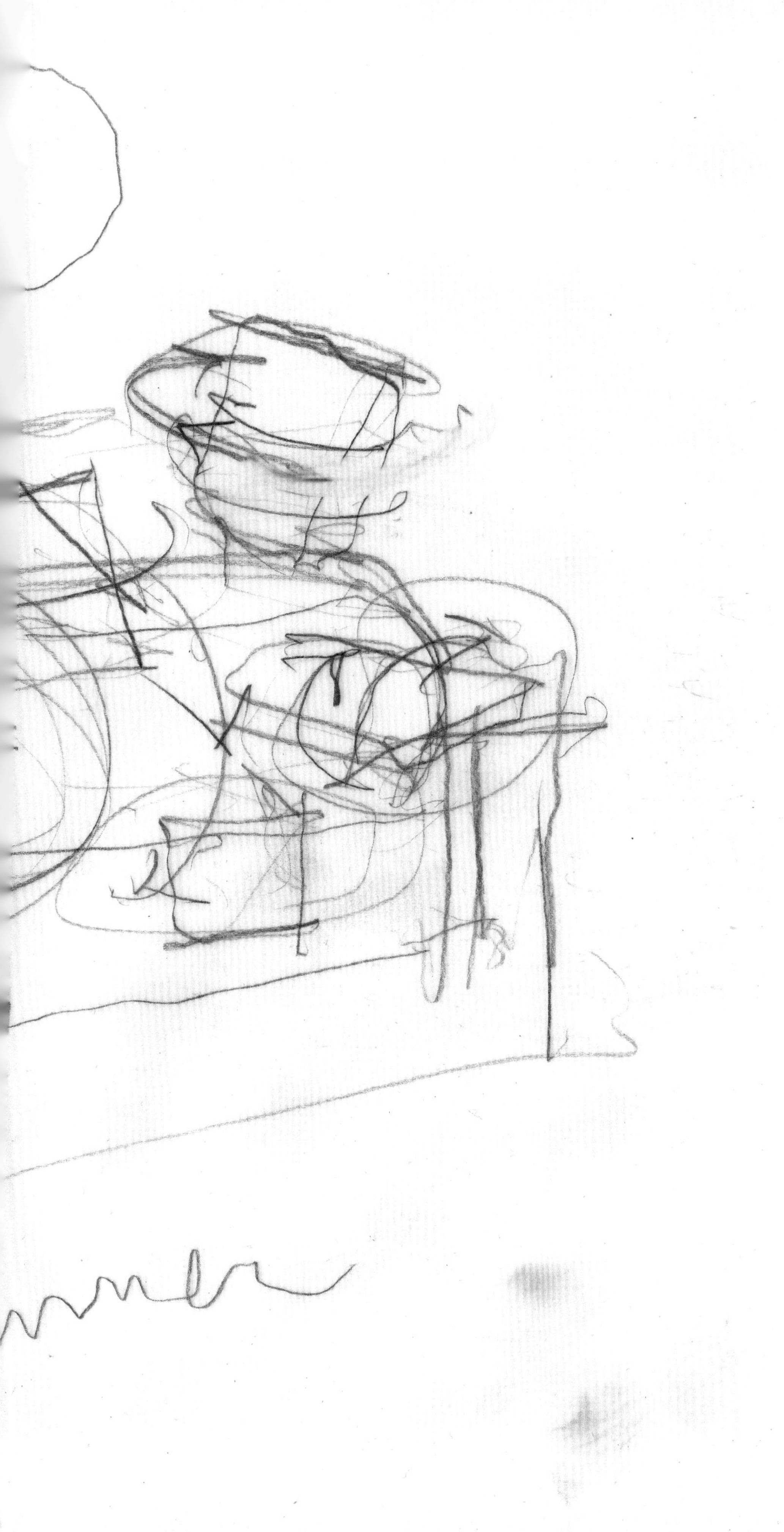

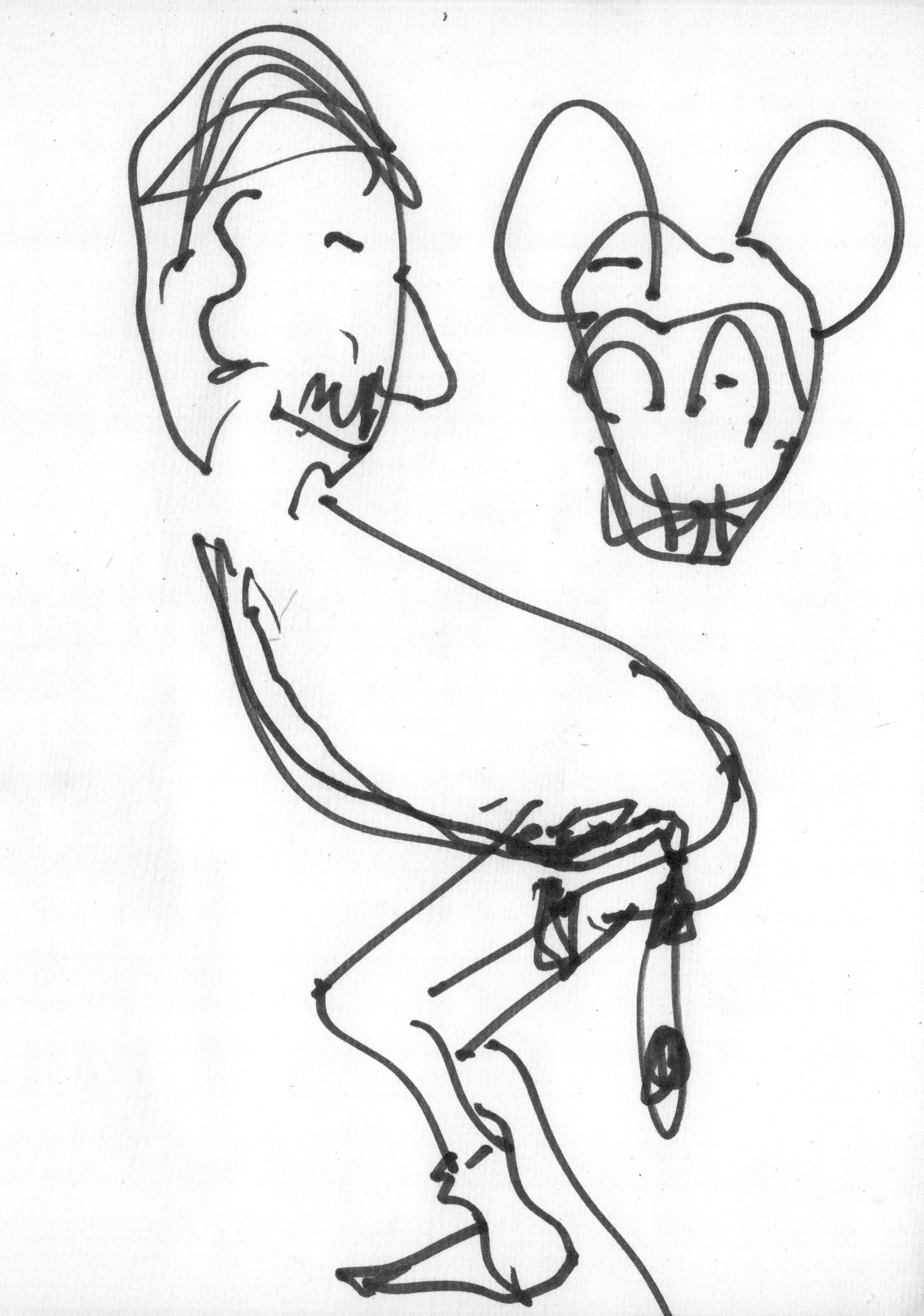

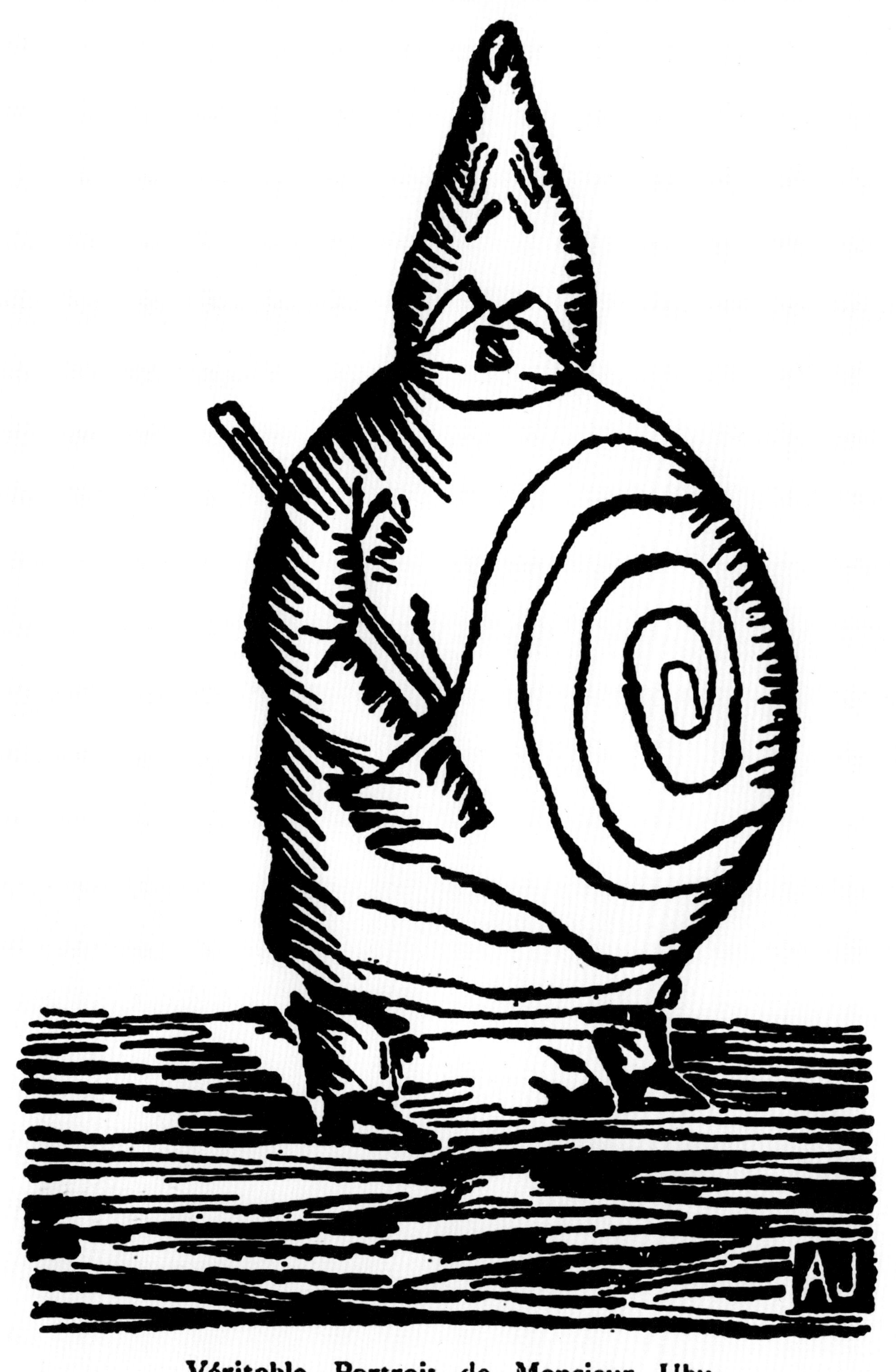

Véritable Portrait de Monsieur Ubu.

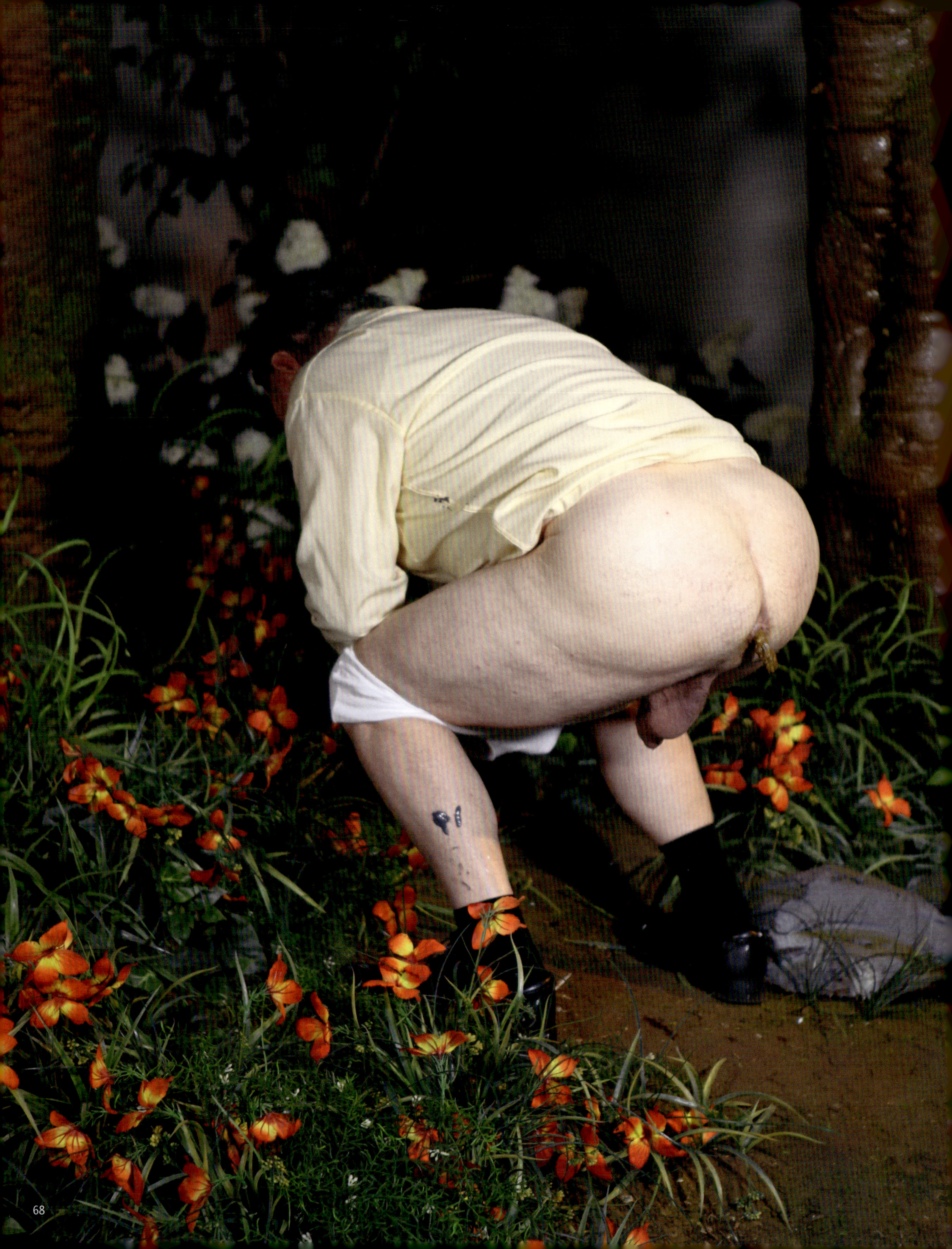

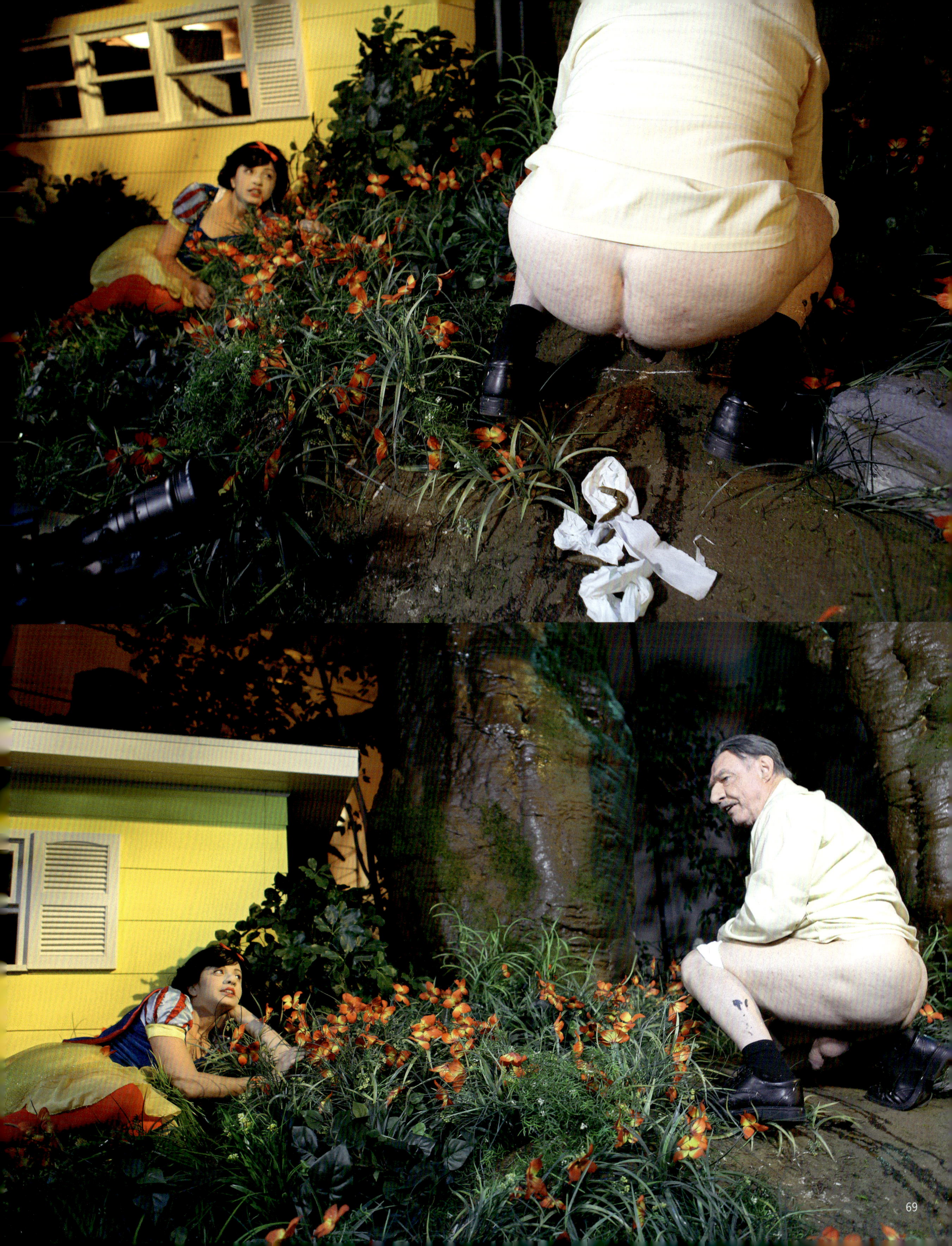

All images courtesy Paul McCarthy and Hauser & Wirth unless otherwise indicated.

Christmas Tree and Village, ca. 1955
Photo by David Love
Archive of Paul McCarthy, p. 3

Needles, 2007
Dead tree, stand, 54 × 58 × 96 in.
Photo by Ann Marie Rounkle, p. 4

Wally Beuys, 1980
Christmas tree with branches cut off, tree stand, 34 × 27 × 86 in.
Photo by Ann Marie Rounkle, p. 5

Platform, 2007
Dead trees, wood, steel drums, mixed media, 60 × 96 × 106 in. (installed dimensions)
Photo by Ann Marie Rounkle, pp. 6–7

Wally Hedrick
Christmas Tree, ca. 1955 (no longer extant)
Mixed media, 72 in. height
Photo credit: Estate of Wally Hedrick
Courtesy of the Estate of Wally Hedrick, p. 8 (upper left)

Page 80 of *Joseph Beuys, Life and Work* by Götz Adriani, Winfried Konnertz, and Karin Thomas (Barron's Educational Series), 1979 [featuring Joseph Beuys, *The Needles of a Christmas Tree*, 1962]
© 2014 Artists Rights Society (ARS), New York / VG Bild-Kunst, Bonn, p. 8 (upper right)

Page 281 of *John Heartfield*: AIZ/ VI 1930–38 by David Evan (Kent Fine Art), 1992 [featuring John Heartfield, *O Christmas Tree in German Soil, How Bent Are Thy Branches*, 1934]
© 2014 Artists Rights Society (ARS), New York / VG Bild-Kunst, Bonn, p. 8 (lower left)

Jay DeFeo
A Room at 2322 Filmore Street, San Francisco, 1958
© 2014 The Jay DeFeo Trust / Artists Rights Society (ARS), New York, p. 9 (lower right)

Santa with Butt Plug Maquette with Tree (Found object, gift from Benjamin Weissman), 2002
Ceramic, 10.5 × 5.75 × 4 in.
Photo by Ann Marie Rounkle, p. 10

Chair with Butt Plug, 1978
Wood chair with rubber "Doc Johnson" butt plug bolted to seat, 35 × 18 × 17 in. (chair)
Photo by Paul McCarthy, p. 11

Butt Plug (Found Object), 2007
Black vinyl, 5 × 3 × 2 in.
Photo by Ann Marie Rounkle, p. 12

Jean Arp
Déméter, 1960
Bronze
Photo by Étienne Bertrand Weill
© 2014 Artists Rights Society (ARS), New York / VG Bild-Kunst, Bonn, p. 13

Jean Arp and Sophie Taeuber
Calice, 1918
Turned wood, painted in polychrome
11.5 in. height
Courtesy Sotheby's
© 2014 Artists Rights Society (ARS), New York / VG Bild-Kunst, Bonn, p. 14

Jean Arp and Sophie Taeuber
Amphore, 1917
Painted wood, 11.8 in. height
© 2014 Artists Rights Society (ARS), New York / VG Bild-Kunst, Bonn, p. 15 (upper left)

Jean Arp
Gur, 1963 / cast 1976/77
Bronze, 38 × 9.2 × 13 in.
Private collection, courtesy Galerie Thomas, Munich
© 2014 Artists Rights Society (ARS), New York / VG Bild-Kunst, Bonn, p. 15 (upper right)

Jean Arp
Appliqué et songeur, 1960
Bronze, polished, 22 × 6.3 × 5.9 in.
Museum Ludwig, Cologne © Rheinisches Bildarchiv Köln, © 2014 Artists Rights Society (ARS), New York / VG Bild-Kunst, Bonn, p. 15 (lower left)

Jean Arp
Demeter's Doll, 1961
Bronze, cast 3/5 (1974)
16.14 × 5.9 × 6.1 in.
Stiftung Arp e.V., Berlin / Rolandswerth
© 2014 Artists Rights Society (ARS), New York / VG Bild-Kunst, Bonn, p. 15 (lower right)

Shit Face Painting, 1974
Gelatin-silver prints & video stills, dimensions variable
Photos by Paul McCarthy, pp. 18–19

Butt Plug, Carbon Fiber, 2009
Carbon fiber (black), 36 × 23.5 × 16 in.
Photo by Fredrik Nilsen, p. 20 (upper left)

Butt Plug, Carbon Fiber, 2009
Carbon fiber (green), 36 × 23.5 × 16 in.
Photo by Fredrik Nilsen, p. 20 (upper right)

Butt Plug, Statuary Marble, 2012
Statuary marble, 35 × 22 × 16 in.
Photo by Stefan Altenburger Photography Zürich, p. 20 (lower left)

Butt Plug, Stainless Steel, 2008
Stainless Steel, 35 × 22 × 16 in.
Photo by Stefan Altenburger Photography Zürich p. 20 (lower right)

Shit Plug, 2002
11-gallon bottle filled with baby oil and dehydrated reconstituted fecal matter collected at Documenta XI, steel cover, plastic barrel, 22 × 11 in., p. 21

Black Plug, Butt Plug, 2007
Installation view at *Air Born Air Borne Air Pressure*, Middelheim Museum, Antwerp, Belgium
Vinyl-coated nylon fabric, fans, rigging, 60 × 30 × 30 ft.
Photo by Niels Donckers, pp. 22–23

Complex Pile, 2007
Installation view at *Air Born Air Borne Air Pressure*, Middelheim Museum, Antwerp, Belgium
Vinyl-coated nylon fabric, fans, rigging, dimensions variable
Photos by Paul McCarthy, pp. 24–25

Installation view of *Santa with Butt Plug, Complex Pile, Piggies, and Black Plug, Butt Plug* at: *Air Pressure*, at De Uithof, Utrecht, Netherlands
Photo by Mark Vos, pp. 26–27

Santa with Butt Plug, Silicone, 2002
Silicone, 44.75 × 23.5 × 18.25 in.
Photo by Ann Marie Rounkle, pp. 28–29

Santa with Butt Plug (Bronze 20'), 2002
Installation view at Basel Unlimited, 2007
Bronze, 244.125 × 118.125 × 128 in., p. 30

Santa with Butt Plug (Fiberglass 20'), 2009–12
Fiberglass (red), 240 × 124 × 120 in.
Photo by Fredrik Nilsen, p. 31

Santa with Butt Plug (Inflatable 80'), 2007
Installation view at *Air Born Air Borne Air Pressure*, Middelheim Museum, Antwerp, Belgium
Vinyl-coated nylon fabric, fans, rigging, 80 × 40 × 40 ft.
Photos by Paul McCarthy, pp. 32–33

Chocolate Factory, NY, 2007
Installation detail at Maccarone Gallery, New York
Photos by Amy Baumann, pp. 34–35

Chocolate Factory, NY, 2007
Installation detail at Maccarone Gallery, New York
Photo by Amy Baumann, p. 36 (top)

Chocolate Factory, NY, 2007
Installation detail at Maccarone Gallery, New York
Photo by Jason Nocito, p. 36 (bottom)

Chocolate Factory, NY, 2007
Installation detail at Maccarone Gallery, New York
Photos by Svetlana Bahchevanova, p. 37

Chocolate Factory, NY, Spinner, 2007
Installation detail at Maccarone Gallery, New York
Photos by Jason Nocito, pp. 38–39

Chocolate Factory, NY, 2007
Installation detail at Maccarone Gallery, New York
Photo by Svetlana Bahchevanova, pp. 40–41

View of Monnaie de Paris's façade from the Seine, Credits Monnaie de Paris, pp. 42–43

View of Monnaie de Paris's façade from the Seine, Credits Monnaie de Paris, p. 44 (top)

View of Peristyle, Monnaie de Paris, Credits Monnaie de Paris, p. 44 (bottom)

View of the Grand Staircase, Monnaie de Paris, Credits Monnaie de Paris, p. 45

View of Salle Guillaume Dupré, Monnaie de Paris, Credits Monnaie de Paris, pp.46–47

Butt Plug Collection (Found Objects, Vinyl)
Dimensions variable
Photos by Dinh Thai, p. 48

Butt Plug Collection (Cast Urethane), 2014
Urethane, dimensions variable
Photos by Alexis Hudgins, p. 49

Santa with Butt Plug and Tree, Chocolate Figurines on Skin: Designs for Ad Layout, 2014
Designed by Louisa Sun McCarthy and Paul McCarthy, pp. 50–51

Chocolate Figurines on Skin: Designs for Poster, 2014
Designed by Louisa Sun McCarthy and Paul McCarthy, pp. 52–53

Digital Rendering for Inflatable Sculpture, Tree, in Place Vendôme, Paris, 2014
Designed by Páll Björnsson and Paul McCarthy, pp. 54–57

Digital rendering of the inflatable sculpture *Santa with Butt Plug* on scaffolding on Place Condorcet, Monnaie de Paris, Credits Monnaie de Paris, p. 58 (upper left)

Digital rendering of the inflatable sculpture *Santa with Butt Plug* in the Courtyard of Honor, Monnaie de Paris, Credits Monnaie de Paris, p. 58 (upper right)

Digital rendering of the inflatable sculpture *Santa with Butt Plug* in the Courtyard of Honor, Monnaie de Paris, Credits Monnaie de Paris, p. 58 (bottom)

Digital rendering for *Plug Grove*, Staircase of Honor, Monnaie de Paris, 2014
Designed by Alex Stevens and Paul McCarthy, p. 59

Carlos' House, Mexican Brothel, 2014
Movie set, dimensions variable
Photos by Páll Björnsson, pp. 60–61

Eiffel Tower and Tree Plug, 2014
Pencil on paper, 15 × 10 in., p. 62

Chocolate Factory Party Life, 2014
Pencil and marker on vellum, 17 × 14 in., p. 63

Spinner, 2014
Pencil on vellum, 11 × 14 in., pp. 64–65

Walt Paul and Mickey Mini, 2014
Marker on paper, 9.75 × 7.5 in., p. 66

Alfred Jarry
Véritable Portrait de Monsieur Ubu, 1896
Woodcut
Frontispiece for *Ubu Roi*, p. 67

WS, 2014
Digital photograph
Photos by Alexis Hudgins, pp. 68–69

This first volume is published on the occasion of Paul McCarthy's solo exhibition *Chocolate Factory,* curated by Chiara Parisi, director of the Cultural Programs department, at Monnaie de Paris from October 25, 2014, to January 4, 2015.

Concept: Paul McCarthy

Graphic design and typesetting: Louisa Sun McCarthy and Paul McCarthy

Production: Julia Günther, Hatje Cantz

Typeface: Apple Chancery, Arial Narrow, Avenir Next Condensed Bold, Helvetica CY Bold, Minion Pro

Paper: BVS matt, 150 g/m^2

Reproductions, printing, and binding: DZA Druckerei zu Altenburg GmbH, Altenburg

Special thanks to:
Monnaie de Paris: Chiara Parisi and Frédéric Legros
Hauser & Wirth: Iwan and Manuela Wirth, Marc Payot, Karin Seinsoth, Stacen Berg, and Nathalie Brambilla
McCarthy Studios: Amy Baumann, Kate Costello, Naotaka Hiro, Georgia Horn, Alexis Hudgins, Dylan Huig,
Damon McCarthy, Karen McCarthy, and Louisa Sun McCarthy

Published by
Hatje Cantz Verlag
Zeppelinstrasse 32
73760 Ostfildern
Germany
Tel. +49 711 4405-200
Fax +49 711 4405-220
www.hatjecantz.com
A Ganske Publishing Group company

Christophe Beaux
Chairman and CEO

Monnaie de Paris
11 Quai de Conti
75006 Paris
France
www.monnaiedeparis.fr

Hatje Cantz books are available internationally at selected bookstores. For more information about our distribution partners, please visit our website at www.hatjecantz.com.

ISBN 978-3-7757-3932-0

Printed in Germany

Cover illustration: *Santa with Butt Plug and Tree, Chocolate Figurines on Skin: Book Cover Design,* 2014
Designed by Louisa Sun McCarthy and Paul McCarthy

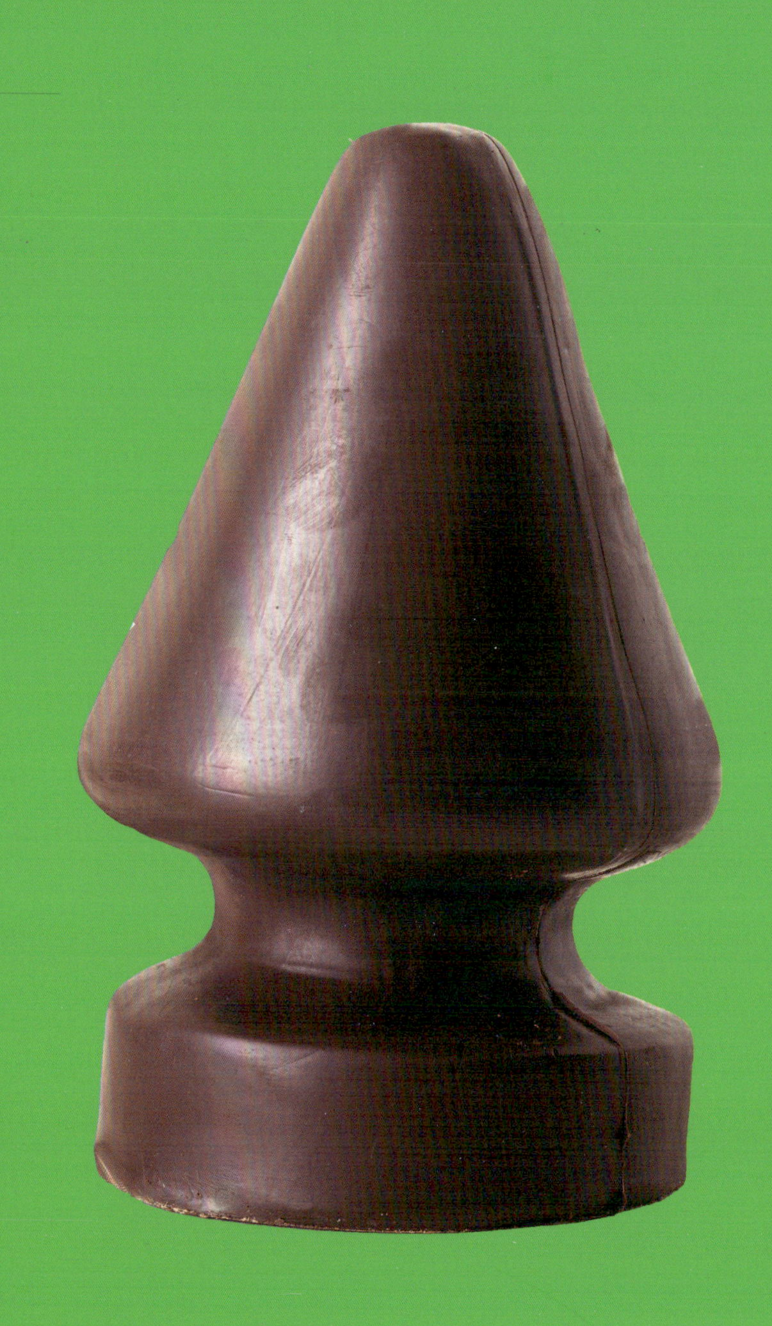